What Is Cultural Criticism?

What Is Cultural Criticism?

Francis Mulhern | Stefan Collini

VERSO
London • New York

First published by Verso 2024
In the collection © Verso Books 2024
Chapters 2, 3, 4, 5, 6, 7 © New Left Review 2024
Chapter 8 © Stefan Collini 2024
'Culture/Metaculture', Francis Mulhern, Copyright © Francis Mulhern
2000, Routledge, reprinted here by kind permission of Taylor & Francis
Group. Reproduced with permission of the Licensor through PLSclear.

The moral rights of the authors have been asserted

1 3 5 7 9 10 8 6 4 2

Verso
UK: 6 Meard Street, London W1F 0EG
US: 388 Atlantic Avenue, Brooklyn, NY 11217
versobooks.com

Verso is the imprint of New Left Books

ISBN-13: 978-1-80429-337-9
ISBN-13: 978-1-80429-339-3 (US EBK)
ISBN-13: 978-1-80429-338-6 (UK EBK)

British Library Cataloguing in Publication Data
A catalogue record for this book is available from the British Library

Library of Congress Cataloging-in-Publication Data

Names: Mulhern, Francis, author. | Collini, Stefan, 1947– author.
Title: What is cultural criticism? / Francis Mulhern, Stefan Collini.
Description: First edition paperback. |
London ; New York : Verso Books,
2024. | Includes bibliographical references and index.
Identifiers: LCCN 2023057873 (print) |
LCCN 2023057874 (ebook) | ISBN
9781804293379 (paperback) | ISBN 9781804293393 (ebk)
Subjects: LCSH: Criticism.
Classification: LCC PN81 .M825 2024 (print)
| LCC PN81 (ebook) | DDC
801.95 – dc23/eng/20240220
LC record available at https://lccn.loc.gov/2023057873
LC ebook record available at https://lccn.loc.gov/2023057874

Typeset in Sabon MT by Hewer Text UK Ltd, Edinburgh
Printed and bound by CPI Group (UK) Ltd, Croydon, CR0 4YY

Contents

Publisher's Note

Argument about culture as a topic has an ancient pedigree. In Britain, figures such as Samuel Taylor Coleridge and Matthew Arnold have come to serve as emblems of longer lineages, while the German tradition of Kulturkritik similarly appealed to the supposedly deeper values embodied in both artistic activity and communal practices. These arguments mingled and expanded in the inter-war era, when comparably emblematic figures included Thomas Mann, T. S. Eliot and F. R. Leavis. Common to these diverse bodies of work was an appeal to the imaginative and intellectual capacities of culture as a critical resource for understanding, challenging, and even partially remedying the ills of modern society.

In the post-war period, Raymond Williams provided an enduring polemical reconstruction of the English line of cultural criticism—though he did not use the term as such—in *Culture and Society* (1958). Williams charged that, for all the strengths of the tradition as a humanist response to industrial capitalism, it depended too much upon an educated elite to produce and diffuse cultural values, rather than broadening the idea of culture to include the meanings produced by working people themselves. Taking that argument further, the project of Cultural Studies developed by Stuart Hall and others aimed to identify the democratic potential inherent in popular self-expression.

At stake in *What Is Cultural Criticism?*, a dialogue between Francis Mulhern and Stefan Collini that first unfolded in the pages of *New Left Review*, is the standing that culture's proponents claim for it in these traditions. The occasion for the exchange was the publication of Mulhern's *Culture/Metaculture* (2000) and

Collini's review of it in *NLR* in 2001. *Culture/Metaculture* registered a fundamental criticism of both Cultural Studies and earlier traditions of 'high' cultural criticism: they tended to discount the validity of the political, the only means by which an alternative order could actually be brought about. Mulhern argued for a different relation between the two practices, a 'cultural politics' that would respect the specificities of each. Reviewing *Culture/ Metaculture* for *NLR*, Collini defended the validity of cultural criticism as a contemporary practice. The debate took off from there, with Mulhern's reply prompting a chain of response and counter-response, the exchange then further extended by recent contributions from both authors.

Mulhern and Collini are among the most consequential thinkers of their generation on these questions, each having made landmark contributions to the understanding of British intellectual culture. Both writers have produced striking portraits of seminal thinkers, as well as more panoramic studies of intellectuals and intelligentsias. Mulhern's *The Moment of 'Scrutiny'*, *Culture/Metaculture* and his comparison of English, French and American intelligentsias in 'Intellectual Identities', republished in *Into the Mêlée*, can be set alongside Collini's *Public Moralists*, *Matthew Arnold* and *Absent Minds: Intellectuals in Britain*. Both have made memorable interventions on current political–cultural issues: Mulhern on the UK's nationalities question, Collini on higher education. Two contrasted formations, then, but also no less striking convergences. Part of what lends the Mulhern–Collini exchange its distinctive character is the fact that, despite the differences between them, their interests have also displayed an almost uncanny kinship or overlap (as Collini remarks at p. 201 below).

The organization of *What Is Cultural Criticism?* is largely self-explanatory. The opening chapter is drawn from the introduction and conclusion to Mulhern's *Culture/Metaculture*, as head text of the debate, followed by Collini's review of it, 'Culture Talk'. In the second section, the debate takes form with Mulhern's reply, 'Beyond Metaculture'; Collini's rejoinder, 'Defending Cultural Criticism'; Mulhern's 'The Logic of Cultural Criticism'; and Collini's concluding 'On Variousness; and on Persuasion'. All were published in *NLR* between 2002 and 2004, generating a broader commentary (see p. 176 below: 'The Naming of Parts', Part III). The final section takes up the discussion a decade and a half later, as Mulhern salutes Collini's long-running public campaign against the marketization of the English university system, and Collini responds with a consideration of Mulhern's latest books, *Figures of Catastrophe* and *Into the Mêlée*, providing his concluding thoughts on the exchange. Rigorous, respectful, forthright, *What Is Cultural Criticism?* offers a genuinely hard-fought debate, in which each protagonist is pressed to clarify and complicate his positions. The outcome is a lasting contribution to arguments within left-democratic cultural theory.

Acknowledgements

Chapter 1: Drawn from the introduction and conclusion to *Culture/Metaculture*, by permission of Routledge.

Chapter 2: First published as 'Culture Talk' in *NLR* 7, Jan.–Feb. 2001.

Chapter 3: First published as 'Beyond Metaculture' in *NLR* 16, July–Aug. 2002.

Chapter 4: First published as 'Defending Cultural Criticism' in *NLR* 18, Nov.–Dec. 2002.

Chapter 5: First published as 'What Is Cultural Criticism?' in *NLR* 23, Sept.–Oct. 2003.

Chapter 6: First published as 'On Variousness; and on Persuasion', *NLR* 27, May–June 2004.

Chapter 7: First published as 'In the Academic Counting-House', *NLR* 123, May–June 2023.

Chapter 8: 'The Naming of Parts', published here for the first time.

I

FRANCIS MULHERN

Culture/Metaculture

Culture has long been said to be a rare and a vulnerable thing, but no one could speak likewise of the discussion it inspires, which, in contrast, has never been more prolific or robust.[1] Familiar modern understandings of the term persist, more or less strongly: culture as a storehouse of essentially human or essentially national values. But they persist now in often radical tension with the newer understanding of culture as the ordinary social, historical world of sense, of 'symbolic' or meaning-bearing activity in all its forms. 'Culture' in that expanded, secular definition has imprinted itself on a whole range of disciplines: history and sociology, for example, and literary studies, where the older meanings have been fundamental, and above all Cultural Studies itself. It follows that no one venturing to add a further volume to the library of contemporary writing in the area should expect the hospitality once readily accorded to travellers from faraway places. Readers will wish to know in what way this book differs from others near to hand. My subject is the discussion itself, 'culture' as a topic in twentieth-century debate, in Europe and particularly in Britain.

A topic, in old, strict usage, is not merely what is spoken of—an object real or imagined: it is an established object of discussion with established terms of treatment. Thus, a topic is always already a convention, implying a settled relationship between those who participate in it. The most successful topics achieve the

---

1 This chapter reproduces the introduction and concluding Part III of Francis Mulhern, *Culture/Metaculture*, London and New York 2000.

status of commonplaces, a metaphor we do well to take literally. In the words of the French sociologist Pierre Bourdieu, they are 'those places in discourse in which an entire group meets and recognizes itself'.[2] The 'place' I wish to explore here is the one called *culture*: that is, 'culture' *as the topic* of some major intellectual traditions of the past century. My own redescription of that topic, which I intend also as a critical displacement of it, is *metaculture*, or *metacultural discourse*. The purpose of the following paragraphs is to introduce these and other key elements in the conceptual vocabulary of the book, and in this way to outline its argument.

Most varieties of discourse identified by the Greek prefix *meta* (literally, 'after' or 'with') will have one and often two distinctive characteristics. They will be concerned with the most general and fundamental problems in their domain—thus, Freud reserved the term 'metapsychology' for his most systematic theoretical accounts of mental life. And they will be more or less strongly reflexive, being themselves a part of what they speak of—thus, 'metafiction' designates a kind of fiction about fiction. Metacultural discourse, then, is that in which culture, however defined, speaks of itself. More precisely, it is discourse in which culture addresses its own generality and conditions of existence. All four terms in this formulation need emphasis. It is the *generality* of sense-making activity that is in question, not merely one or another of its many specific varieties, say, religious worship or window-shopping or poetry or adult education. That generality is addressed in its social-historical *conditions of existence*, which may be conceptualized, for example, as 'industrialism', or 'capitalism', or 'modernity'. Metaculture is *discourse* in the strong sense of that versatile term: a historically formed set of topics and procedures that both drives and regulates the utterance of the individuals who inhabit it, and assigns them definite positions in the field of meaning it delimits. The position of seeing and speaking and writing in metacultural discourse, the kind of subject any individual 'becomes' in practising it, is *culture itself*. There will

---

2   Pierre Bourdieu, *The Field of Cultural Production*, ed. and Introduction, Randal Johnson, Oxford 1993, p. 168.

be more to say shortly. For now, let me stress that no one, to my knowledge, has ever described themselves as a practitioner of 'metacultural discourse'. The term and the concept have emerged from the critical work of writing this book. If any one term or reference or affiliation might be said to link all the writers discussed here—and in bare truth there is none—it would be the more familiar *culture*.

One term, but hardly one meaning—the very phrase 'culture itself' seems unwarrantable. 'Culture' has designated quite distinct and sometimes mutually foreign fields of practice and inquiry, and has graced the banners of radically opposed causes. The largely chronological sequencing of this book, from 1918 to the near-present, does not imply a simple narrative of progress (or decline). Its main principle of organization is comparative, foregrounding two mutually antagonistic traditions of discourse on culture— Kulturkritik and Cultural Studies—terms that must themselves be clarified here. The first is much older. The second took shape in conscious opposition to it. But my chief critical interest lies in the evidence of continuity between them, in the conceptual *form* they appear to have in common. Here is the sense in which the singular 'culture itself' is perhaps not so ambiguous after all.

The German term *Kulturkritik* passes literally into English as 'cultural criticism'. However, this simple translation creates conceptual confusion. The English phrase is in widespread use as a general term denoting any kind of formal discussion of any activity thought of as cultural: literary criticism, film reviews, fashion commentaries of a certain kind, or homilies on contemporary sexual mores are so many instances of cultural criticism in this familiar, spacious sense. However, the historical meaning of Kulturkritik is much narrower. For that reason—for the sake of simplicity, in fact—I have preferred to import it directly (and to print it, henceforward, without its foreignizing italics) as a term that is both adequately general and properly restrictive, and thus critically exact. Kulturkritik, in its classic European form, took shape in the later eighteenth century as a critical, normally negative discourse on the emerging symbolic universe of capitalism, democracy and enlightenment—on the values of a condition and process of social life for which a recent French coinage furnished the essential term: *civilisation*.[3] Germany was the continental heartland of this discourse: it was in the philosophical histories of Johann Gottfried von Herder that *Zivilisation* was first questioned in the name of Kultur.[4] The second major European centre of Kulturkritik was England, whose counterpart tradition is the subject of Raymond Williams's classic study, *Culture and Society*. 'The basic element' in this discourse, Williams concluded there, 'is its effort at total qualitative assessment . . . of the whole form of our common life'—or what I have termed the 'generality' of symbolic life and its historical 'conditions of existence'.[5] The critical resources for that effort were confirmed by the poet Matthew Arnold, in the 1860s, as 'culture'. Culture, for Arnold, was a normative value: it was 'the best which has been thought and said in the world', 'the passion for sweetness and light', 'the study of perfection', harmonious and general; it was 'right reason' concerned to 'know the object as in itself it really is'.[6] Although developmental in character, culture was universal in its moral scope and application, emerging from and directed towards what was distinctively human in humanity, the 'best self' that might qualify and even overrule the 'ordinary selves' of everyday class and other social interests. It was the spiritual basis of a possible civil order, as binding in its sphere, and, ideally, as commanding as the state itself.[7] Culture, in this construction, is not merely a repository of value: it is the *principle* of a good society. Arnold's statement of the cultural principle, as it can pointedly be called, became classic in English-language Kulturkritik in the twentieth century.[8] Yet his

---

3 Lucien Febvre, *A New Kind of History*, Peter Burke, ed., London 1973, pp. 219–57.

4 Johann Gottfried von Herder, *Herder on Social and Political Culture*, ed. and trans. F. M. Barnard, Cambridge 1969 [1774], pp. 179–224.

5 Raymond Williams, *Culture and Society 1780–1950*, Harmondsworth 1961 [1958], p. 285.

6 Matthew Arnold, *Culture and Anarchy*, J. Dover Wilson, ed., Cambridge 1932 [1869].

7 For an illuminating discussion, see David Lloyd and Paul Thomas, *Culture and the State*, London 1998.

8 Dover Wilson's scholarly 1932 edition of Arnold's *Culture and Anarchy* (1869) was the first of its kind; the journal *Scrutiny*, which was launched in Cambridge in the same year, 1932, pursued an avowedly Arnoldian cultural strategy; the USA's leading Arnoldian, Lionel Trilling, published his biography, *Matthew Arnold*, in 1939.

assumption that the norms of culture were necessarily those of universal humanity is not typical of the tradition more widely seen. Herder, too, valued *Humanität* and its development, but the 'culture' that mediated that 'human-ness' was, for him, always in reality plural and historically relative. Cultures were the symbolic forms of life of human groups, shaped in diverse conditions and growing into new shapes as they encountered new demands and opportunities. The civilizing process could not, or should not, uproot these equally though differently 'human' cultures, whose most important emerging variety was the nation. 'Human nature is not the vessel of an absolute, unchanging and independent happiness, as defined by the philosopher ... Even the image of happiness changes with each condition and climate ... each nation has its centre of gravity within itself, just as every sphere has its centre of gravity.'[9] Here, too, is the cultural principle. Of course, this romantic counter-emphasis on culture-as-national-value, as the 'traditional' virtue of a people, seems incompatible with Arnold's humanism. But intellectual history does not follow the rules of logic textbooks, and, as we shall see, twentieth-century Kulturkritik sustained both varieties of 'culture' and produced hybrids of the two, all of them sharing a single discursive form.

The greater historical impact of Herder's thought was regis-tered elsewhere, however, in the emergence of an array of discourses on 'culture' as what T. S. Eliot would call 'a whole way of life'. The world-transforming power of nationalism, from the mid-nineteenth century into our continuing present, has ensured the universal currency of 'culture' in this sense—as, in effect, ethnic custom. In the field of formalized intellectual inquiry, its main sponsor, until the later twentieth century, was anthropology. 'Cultural' or 'social' anthropology, the settled names for a pursuit first proposed as simple 'culturology', took shape as the putative science of the 'superorganic': of learned rather than instinctive behaviour, or, more strictly, the 'symboling' life of societies.[10] 'Culture' in this sense might indeed be valued (according to the lights and purposes of the visiting anthropologist) but it was not,

9 Herder, *Herder on Social and Political Culture*, pp. 185–6.
10 L. A. White, *The Concept of Cultural Systems*, New York 1975.

in Arnold's general sense, a normative value, a precious human endowment of spiritual capital. It was the totality of symbolic life in a given social space. Anthropology itself lies beyond the range of this study. However, Eliot's phrase is only one among many illustrations of its exemplary status in the wider intellectual life of the past century, and, specifically, of the inspirational value it was assigned in the formation of a new discourse on culture in mid-century Britain—what came to be called cultural studies. That lineage of cultural studies (which, in this book, I spell with initial capitals, except where my intended reference is not only to the academic practice so named) emerged in a complex process that was both a continuation and a displacement of English Kulturkritik. The theoretical stakes in that process play a major part in what follows here, and for now I will indicate only as much as may serve to move these introductory remarks towards their conclusion. Cultural studies has evolved more than once.[11] It has more or less established positions throughout the English-speaking world, and has now extended its reach well beyond them. Its niche, it seems, is the planet. The critical account I develop here is based on the British case, which, I know, is not the beginning and end of all possible cultural studies. At the same time, that variety has thus far enjoyed greater international currency than any other, and even if it has no special claim to global authority, its record deserves particular attention. For the same reason, the arguments advanced here have implications reaching beyond the British setting.

Cultural Studies has favoured a radical expansion of the field of relevant inquiry, and a strictly egalitarian ethic of attention within it. Any form or practice of signification is in principle eligible, without any presumptive test of 'quality'. But these are studies with a mission that is not merely sociological or anthropological. The justifying purpose of Cultural Studies has been to revoke the historic privileges of 'culture with a capital C' (the sovereign value

---

11   James W. Carey, 'Reflections on the Project of (American) Cultural Studies', in Marjorie Ferguson and Peter Golding, eds, *Cultural Studies in Question*, London 1997; John Frow and Meaghan Morris, 'Australian Cultural Studies', in Valda Blundell, John Shepherd and Ian Taylor, eds, *Relocating Cultural Studies*, London 1993.

of Kulturkritik) and vindicate the active meanings and values of the subordinate majority (the so-called masses) as core elements of a possible alternative order. 'Power' is indissociable from meaning, in this perspective, which is thus necessarily 'political'.[12] My argument will be that Cultural Studies is prone to misrecognize itself: that its predominant tendency has been to negate the specific social values of Kulturkritik while retaining their deep form, which it therefore repeats as the pattern of its own strategic imagination. The coordinates of that form are *culture*, *authority* and *politics*.

In both versions, *culture* is the object but also, and crucially, the subject, the ideal subject, of discourse. It is the cultural principle itself (be it elite or popular) that furnishes the conditions of seeing and speaking, that determines what I see and speak of, and as what 'I' do so. In keeping with this, the cultural principle also sets the conditions of ethically valid intellectual practice: metacultural discourse is normally, among other things, a reflection on the meaning of intellectual vocation. The ultimate stake, in all cases, is social *authority*. 'Power', in the indiscriminate sense that has been standard in Cultural Studies, is a blunt instrument of scant theoretical value here. Injunctive social practices—those of command and control in the broadest senses—take a variety of forms, including the sanctions deriving from the ownership and control of property and, at the extreme, physical coercion, for which the term 'power' is perhaps best reserved. Cultural injunction is typically not of that kind: its dominant mode is *authority*, which is itself predominantly cultural in substance. Authority relations are those in which assent is secured on non-coercive grounds. The mark of authority, as a form of injunction, is that it normally appears as if granted by those who defer to it. Metacultural discourse lodges a polemical authority claim of the most general kind, in respect of social relations as a whole: the cultural principle is the basis of public virtue. The socially contrasted ideal subjects of Kulturkritik and Cultural Studies are alike in this: both urge 'culture' as the necessary, unregarded truth

---

12 Stuart Hall, 'Culture and Power' (interview), *Radical Philosophy* 86, November–December 1997.

of society, whose curse is the inadequacy of the prevailing form of general authority, *the political*. It is politics as such that is fundamentally in question here: in declared principle, in the case of Kulturkritik, or as a self-defeating final implication, in the case of Cultural Studies. The latter's 'political' assault on high-cultural privilege has turned out to be, at the same time, a renewed attempt at a 'cultural' dissolution of politics—a popular-leftist mutation of metacultural discourse.

The evidence for these bald claims and the elaborated, more nuanced arguments they depend upon are the substance of *Culture/Metaculture*. Part I begins with a discussion of European Kulturkritik in its diverse national sensibilities and intellectual formats. The novelist Thomas Mann, the philosophers Julien Benda and José Ortega y Gasset, the sociologist Karl Mannheim and the literary critic F. R. Leavis are brought together as classic critics of 'mass' modernity between the First and Second World Wars. Sigmund Freud, Virginia Woolf, George Orwell and assorted Marxisms then illustrate the stresses to which the common assumptions of such criticism were subject in the 1930s. T. S. Eliot and Richard Hoggart define the new terms of cultural reflection in post-war Britain. The crucial work of Raymond Williams enables a critical retrospect on the tradition of Kulturkritik and the break into a new way of theorizing culture. Cultural studies, broadly understood, is the second major tradition discussed here. Part II reconstructs the conceptual formation of Cultural Studies, focusing particularly on the British tradition. Stuart Hall and his collaborators at the Birmingham Centre for Cultural Studies come to the fore here, in discussions of media analysis, contemporary politics, ethnicity, Marxism and the controversy over 'populism' in the analysis of culture. Throughout this discussion of Cultural Studies, my critical priority is to elicit its discoverable relations with Kulturkritik, the tradition it has struggled against, and to elucidate its opaque ambivalence towards the tradition of theory and politics to which it owes its existence, namely Marxism. The unifying theme of Parts I and II is the relationship between culture, in its conflicting senses, and the idea of politics. The concluding part of the book is devoted to a general analysis, both formal and historical, of the logic of metaculture—the utopian impulse, common to the old cultural criticism and the new cultural studies, to resolve the tension of the relationship between culture and politics by dissolving political reason itself.

Seen as a whole, then, the book is historical in procedure: meta-cultural discourse is understood as an entity shaped and reshaped in determinate social conditions. Its governing question is critical. What has been the form and logic of that discourse and how far is it valid? The form of that question, which is general, in turn dictates the thematic proportions of the book: the older and newer preoccupations of Kulturkritik and Cultural Studies—the large issues of markets, classes, gender, sexuality, race and post-coloniality, to name the most salient ones—are present here, but not as independent headings of discussion. There are many books that offer a tour of the syllabus in their field, but this is not one of them. I emphasize this point, believing that there are few easier paths into difficulty than the one paved with fixed expectations.

Critical commentaries are as much works in themselves as the texts they discuss—they may be worthless, but that is another question—and cannot seriously be offered, or safely be taken, as labour-saving substitutes for them. And when, as in this case, the individual commentaries function as stages in a single, continuous argument, the order of reading becomes crucial. The book has been written as a considered whole, and asks to be read as such, in its given sequence—which, indeed, is the most accessible way through it.

The record of European Kulturkritik in the twentieth century bears witness to its force: its power of attraction as a way of evaluating modernity, and—no less impressive—its ability to absorb radical challenges to its presumptive truth. The cultural studies tradition took shape in radical opposition to Kulturkritik, but my critical claim has been that there, too, metacultural discourse has remained tendentially dominant. That is, it has not simply been the dominant tendency, but the discourse that spontaneously tends to dominate. Such an assertion is inevitably controversial. Actually-existing Cultural Studies is a heterogeneous formation. Intellectual purity has never been seen as a rule to observe or a goal to attain in its strategies of self-development, and the pragmatic conditions of late-century academic existence have in fact tended to favour rather than frustrate this preference. (The discipline is better adapted to its environment than its devotees or their traditionalist detractors like to think.) Yet throughout this impure formation there runs a critical differential, a theme that marks off the idea of Cultural Studies proper from the various theories and methods that support the teaching and research programmes carried on in its name. What has distinguished this project-discipline from the ordinary run of theories and sociologies of culture is its impulse to create its analytic object as a subject: to establish what is spoken of as the entity that speaks of it. Thus, it seeks to validate a new cultural subject, and, in final effect, to institute culture as the authoritative subject of a discourse on social relations.

Culture, here, is more than a corpus of forms and practices, however radically extended in range. It is more even than the social whole seen in its signifying aspect: as in Kulturkritik, it is the principle, the condition of valid social judgement. Benda's eternal truths, Mann's nation and Leavis's human values were variant embodiments of this indivisible authority, in the name of which they uttered their critiques of modern social particularism, and, above all, of those interests they associated with 'mass' existence. Cultural Studies has displaced the notion of the mass for the sake of the subaltern popular, and therewith discomposed the authoritative subject of Kultur in the interest of a radical alternative. But in doing so much yet no more, it has reproduced the discursive form of what it seeks to overcome. The stake is not the scope of what is held to be 'culture', or the pattern of social values inscribed in it—as if the old Kulturkritik were at fault only in its narrowness and traditionalism. What is at issue here is that principle. It is the *status* of the cultural, and specifically its relation to the established form of general social authority, namely politics. Kulturkritik did not doubt its entitlements: politics is inherently deficient as a mode of general authority, which can emerge only from the elusive life of the whole, or culture. Cultural Studies could scarcely recognize itself in such terms, but nevertheless so it has spoken, constituting itself as a permanent rebuke to the upstart authorities of 'the left'. If the *p*-word in Cultural Studies discourse often seems as empty as it is insistent, this is because the desire that powers it is, in the context, unspeakable. Culture, now popular and opposi-tional, and represented by the 'organic intellectuals' of the new project-discipline, takes over the prerogatives once vested in another kind of intellectual. Metacultural discourse is metapoli-tics, the be-all and end-all of (left) political reason.

The Desire Called Cultural Studies

How might this uncanny phenomenon be accounted for?[13] Cultural Studies has become a part of its own corpus in recent years, as commentators explore the logic of its emergence and tendencies of development, laying special emphasis on its imme-diate social and political contexts. Jim McGuigan notes its specific appeal for those without secure social antecedents for their identity as intellectuals—first-generation working-class graduates, and 'in general . . . those from positions of social subordination and marginality'.[14] He also notes the formative pressure of a more concentrated sectoral interest, a new 'class fraction', neither bourgeois nor intellectual in anterior senses, but implanted now in culturally central practices of 'presentation and representation'—the media and the publicity industry. Out of this determinate historical configuration, he suggests, comes 'the populist intervention in cultural knowledge' that is Cultural Studies, and which 'can be understood, in the first instance, as a . . . struggle for symbolic power, representing fairly narrow inter-ests yet similarly evincing a certain democratization of culture: a postmodern populism'.[15] Uncritical populism thus appears as an inborn behavioural propensity, in which 'solidarity' tends to degenerate into 'sentimentality', which is in effect a kind of social conformism. John Fiske's notions of semiotic democracy, of tele-vision as a liberated cultural zone, are 'homologous' with the

---

13   The subtitle of this section borrows a phrase from Fredric Jameson, 'On "Cultural Studies"', *Social Text* 34, 1993, a review essay on Lawrence Grossberg et al., *Cultural Studies*, London 1992.

14   Jim McGuigan, *Cultural Populism*, London 1992, pp. 11–12.

15   Ibid., p. 220.

neoliberal dogma of consumer choice, McGuigan observes. They are a mock-oppositional replay of the leading ideology in contemporary capitalism.

This sociological hypothesis coexists with a critical judgement of uncertain explanatory status, concerning, as it happens, the fading of explanation as an intellectual value in Cultural Studies. McGuigan condemns the growing preference for sympathetic interpretation as a priority in the analysis of popular consumption, and the corresponding want of attention to the structural conditions of cultural practices, and calls for a reunification of interpretive and explanatory forms of inquiry. But, beyond this, he is also tempted to consider this partitioning of theory and method as a causal factor in the growth of 'uncritical populism'. Todd Gitlin, on the other hand, although writing in a spirit akin to McGuigan's, sees in the narrative of Cultural Studies the imprint of a specifically political history. Gitlin endorses the formative ambitions of Cultural Studies in its own customary terms. He seconds early New Left perceptions of the increasing social weight of popular culture in post-war capitalism, and of the unfamiliar, perhaps politically significant collective subjectivities taking form within it. But he is correspondingly astringent in his assessment of the new project-discipline as it evolved in the political conjunctures of the 1970s and 1980s. Cultural Studies, he writes,

> is a form of intellectual life that answers to passions and hopes imported into its precincts from outside. Cultural studies may not be a significant social movement beyond the precincts of certain academies [Gitlin is alluding here to a characteristically grandiose claim on behalf of the discipline], but it certainly responds to the energies of social and cultural movements—and their eclipse.[16]

Gitlin's thesis is that the political claims of Cultural Studies have developed in inverse proportion to the actual political fortunes of

16   Todd Gitlin, 'The Anti-political Populism of Cultural Studies', in Ferguson and Golding, *Cultural Studies in Question*, pp. 25–6.

the wider left of which it has been a part. It has fashioned itself as a redemptive substitute for blocked or defeated movements:

> Perhaps it was youth culture that would inaugurate, cement, ennoble the rising class that inevitably would displace and over-come the ruling groups! At least popular culture had vitality, rebelliousness, oppositional spirit—and then, by implication, so could the people who made it popular. If political power was fore-closed, the battlements of culture still remained to be taken! Or perhaps—if one really believed that the personal was political—they had already been taken. Or perhaps the only reason politics looked unavailing was that the wrong culture was in force.[17]

More sympathetic, for all his broad parody, than McGuigan, Gitlin is equally severe in his judgement on Cultural Studies conformism, and not at all academicist in his sense of the neces-sary corrective:

> [Is] there a chance of a modest redemption? Perhaps, if we imagine a harder-headed, less wishful cultural studies, free of the burden of imagining itself to be a political practice. A chas-tened, realistic cultural studies would divest itself of political pretensions. It would not claim to *be* politics . . . It would be less romantic about the world but also about itself. Less would be more.[18]

The *p*-word, no longer compulsively uttered, might recover some of its critical force.

Between Past and Future

McGuigan's sociological conjecture and Gitlin's political reading furnish important elements of an understanding of Cultural Studies. In themselves, however, they lack both specificity and

---

17 Ibid., p. 29.
18 Ibid., p. 37.

generality. A fully concrete account would have to be strictly comparative, neither assuming the world-defining significance of the British experience nor reducing the ambiguities of its singular international effectivity. At the same time—and this is the crucial consideration in this setting of argument—it would not mistake local specificity for uniqueness in time and space. It would not defer to the assumption—which is that of Cultural Studies itself— that the discursive formation to be explained is a novelty, or only a novelty, a recent creation of distinctively recent conditions. Gitlin accepts this assumption, if only by default, with the interesting result that his perceptions exceed the terms of his explanation. The specificities of the 1970s cannot have given rise to a phenomenon that long predates them. The cultural impulse 'to *be* politics' is older and more general. 'The anti-political populism of Cultural Studies', as Gitlin terms it, seems less a development, be it for good or for ill, than a case of persistence, if not regressive fixation; a paradoxical episode in the history of metaculture. It is this discursive formation, not the record of Cultural Studies, which is only one of its sites of elaboration, that is centrally in question here.

'The working-out of the idea of culture', Raymond Williams once wrote, 'is a slow reach again for control.'[19] The placing of *control*, at the close of both a sentence and a paragraph in the concluding chapter of *Culture and Society*, marks its critical importance. There is more to say about this (though it is worth noting at once that in English, compared with other languages sharing the Latin original, the word can be ambiguous, semantically associated not merely with *checking* or *monitoring* but also with the far stronger meanings of *dominance* or *command*). But first, however, we should pause to consider the temporality here inscribed in 'the idea of culture'. The 'working-out' and the 'slow reach' imply a progressive movement towards a point of transcendence, in which a persisting condition—the reach is slow—is negated. But into the phrasing of this temporality Williams inserts the stylistically awkward *again*, thus invoking a second, distinct temporality in which the future becomes the moment of recovery,

---

19   Williams, *Culture and Society*, p. 285.

the making good not merely of lack but of loss. The functioning of these distinct temporalities in metacultural discourse is complex in the strict sense: neither is the inner truth of the other, and they vary to extremes, from case to case, in their relative force. It is the more interesting, then, that Williams, who knew this, should nevertheless have emphasized their joint implication in a single historical practice.

Intuitions of loss define the temporal imagination of Kulturkritik. Be it of a whole national mentality (Mann) or of a rarefied spiritual discipline (Benda), of political or cultural order (Ortega, Leavis) or of a cohesive social scheme of perception and interest (Mannheim), the loss is always one of integral authority. The past is the standard from which modernity has erred, and the pattern—if there is one—of adjustment. For Mann and Benda, the only strategic options were personal, the ethical disciplines of irony or contemplation. Ortega turned to prophecy. Leavis and Mannheim canvassed activist solutions in the public sphere. All substantiated their claims to critical integrity in imageries of aristocracy or priesthood, the historic types of a general authority they would honour as recusants in exile or, deceptively, as a new meritocracy in the face of the modern iconoclasts. Mannheim and Leavis coupled the temporalities of transcendence and recovery in efficient schemes of cultural substitution, in which new educational elites would recover something of the authority of old hierarchies. (Eliot, the settled reactionary, perceived as much, and stiffened his defences accordingly: Kultur was not, in truth, best served by Kritik, which might educate a Cromwell—or, at any rate, a Hoggart.) For another pair, Woolf and Orwell, no such discursive finesse was available. They wrote in solidarity with subaltern social interests—those of women and workers, respectively—that could not easily be sublimated into an ideal community of the mind, a location that neither of them was, in any case, pre-adapted to occupy. The double temporality of 'culture' worked here, too, producing visions of emancipation but also a damaging ambivalence. Woolf drew on the literary past for her image of an androgynous future, but was also drawn back to it, as a time before the onset of feminist agitation and a crisis-ridden 'sex consciousness'.[20] Orwell called for a socialist revolution powered by a national-popular England—which was, however, the spiritual base from which he launched his own rhetorical insurrections against his fellow intellectuals of the left.

The later tradition of metaculture has dispensed with all such temporal couplings, efficient or not. If Eliot, in his conservatism, exemplified the flat rejection of social transcendence, seeking only to confirm inherited cultural inequality, his true antithesis is Cultural Studies, which incarnates the will to negation in the interests of emancipatory change. *No longer* . . . is the time signal of the discipline. The past is that which must (now) be repudiated, be it Kulturkritik or a certain Marxist economism, which in this discourse appear as strict complements, both figuring the annulment of popular creativity. Or—for the axiom is reversible—that which is to be repudiated must for that very reason be rendered as past, even at the cost of apparent self-contradiction: the temporalizing rhetoric of Stuart Hall's commentary on New Times is an epitome of this. The typical Cultural Studies subject—the practitioner as advocate of the disciplinary project—itself enacts this compulsive modernism, always announcing itself as if for the first time, shedding what it would otherwise have to assume as a formative, therefore limiting, history, a past of one's own. At a comfortable extreme—which, as the cases of Iain Chambers and Dick Hebdige illustrate, is not merely hypothetical—this modernism is indeed objectively conformist. A certain kind of organic intellectual reverses Eliot's traditionalism and lives the present as though it were the desirable future—which, once it has been conjured into actuality in this way, ceases to exist as a critical force capable of passing judgement on what actually exists. However, to insist onesidedly on the banalizing effect of such gestures would itself be an act of banalization. Metacultural discourse in the left-modernist variation that is Cultural Studies incarnates the impulse to accelerate Williams's slow reach for control, a utopian desire to be—actually *be*—one step ahead of its own validating historical process.

---

20 Compare her historical fantasy *Orlando* (1928), in which the androgynous protagonist cannot forget the man s/he nearly met, who may have been Shakespeare.

Metaculture and Society

The motifs of 'acceleration' and measured anticipation (a practice '*one* step ahead' of its own process) come from the days of Thomas Mann's *Reflections*. Their source is a lecture given by the Marxist critic and philosopher Georg Lukács in June 1919, in his capacity as a commissar for education and culture in the Hungarian revolutionary government.[21] The urgent purpose of the lecture, 'The Changing Function of Historical Materialism', was to define the specificity of socialist revolution and, in particular, to vindicate the role of 'violence', the moment of deliberate force in political practice, in its making. However, as the title suggests, Lukács built his case from arguments of the most general kind, which, it will quickly emerge, go to the heart of the question of metacultural discourse.[22] His fundamental theoretical intent was a critique of 'economics'. The historical achievement of capitalism, and its difference as a system from all its predecessors, he maintained, lay in its unprecedented power to transform the given material world, to transcend 'natural limits'.[23] Yet in the same measure, the specifically social relations and objectives that would henceforward be historically dominant themselves assumed the special, apparently natural form of 'economics', a social form in which the realities so designated appeared, along with law and the state, as a '*closed*' system, an apparatus 'apparently quite independent, hermetic and autonomous'.[24] Marx had classically criticized the 'vulgar' economists who abstracted the capitalist market from its constitutive social relations and eternalized it as economic nature. Now, Lukács argued, vulgar Marxism had done likewise, mistaking the

---

21   As Lukács wrote years later, this was the period in which he and Mann parted spiritual company, Mann continuing in the romantic-pessimist tradition that had formed them both. Georg Lukács, *Essays on Thomas Mann*, London 1964, p. 10.

22   Indeed, that problem was Lukács's own. Just a year earlier he had published an essay on 'The Old Culture and the New Culture', which attempted to synthesize a romantic critique of 'civilization' with his new-found belief in the redemptive potential of social revolution.

23   Georg Lukács, *History and Class Consciousness*, London 1971, p. 233.

24   Ibid., p. 230.

specifically capitalist form of economic life for an anthropological constant, a 'law' of history. The laws of economic nature, be that eternal or evolutionary, were indices of alienated social relations. In cancelling the reality, revolution would also 'annul' the law. The moment of 'socialization', Lukács declared, entails a restructuring of property relations but also, and in consequence of that, a transformation of the status of 'the economic' within the social whole. It involves *a turning in the direction of something qualitatively new*, that is, 'conscious action directed towards the comprehended totality of society'. Violence—or mass revolutionary politics—breaks 'the hold of reified relations over man and the hold of economics over society', and clears the approach to a state of things in which 'ideology' becomes the dominant, 'the authentic content of human life'.[25]

If Lukács's prospectus seems to us to evince a richly period quality, that is a reflection on our own historical parochialism. The problem he tackled here is that of metaculture itself. The theme of 'economics' will be familiar to any reader of Raymond Williams and Stuart Hall as that of 'base and superstructure'—indeed Williams, in an independent parallel development of thought, constructed his own critique in the same substantive terms.[26] However, with greater lucidity than either, Lukács associated the theoretical crux of economic determinism with the politico-cultural crux of deliberative authority (the idea of 'a consciously directed society'[27]), and proposed an integrated solution to them. Economic determinism is not so much pure error, Lukács argued in effect, as a false generalization from the historically distinctive reality of capitalism, which constitutes 'the economic' as a specialized, autonomous process and favours corresponding forms of social reason—'economics'. The necessary corollaries for a society thus governed by 'economic compulsion' are an instrumentalized politics (a form of governance based on submission to an

---

25   Ibid., pp. 250–2.
26   See *The Long Revolution*, Part I, and, quite generally, *Marxism and Literature*, where ideas akin to those of Lukács's *History and Class Consciousness* are central.
27   Lukács, *History and Class Consciousness*, p. 251.

intractable real world) and an ineffectual culture (valued but useless 'principles that [can] occur only as "superstructure"', as secondary, dependent). In other words, a structurally induced enfeeblement of authority and power of social deliberation. In this, too, capitalism differs constitutionally from preceding and succeeding forms of society. Although Lukács did not say so much, it is consistent with his analysis to recall the fatalistic discourses of social authority—religious or traditionalist—that transfigured the 'natural limits' of feudalism. He was of course emphatic in his conviction that socialism could outstrip not only 'natural limits' but those of 'economics and violence' as well, creating the conditions of a politics consisting in what had 'until now' been 'merely "Ideology"'—or culture.

The historical context of Lukács's argument was socialist revolution, achieved (in Russia) or in progress (in his native Hungary and elsewhere in Central Europe). It is capitalism that must concern us here. Lukács's basic claim, in its first, Marxian form, is that the capitalist mode of production is necessarily anarchic, in the strongest sense: it is finally ungovernable.[28] Yet the epoch of capitalism has also been that of politics, the locus and means of the struggle for social self-determination according to one or another available formulation of that distinctively modern end: liberty, democracy, independence, equality, welfare, socialism. Bourgeois civilization has exalted politics in socio-economic conditions that sooner or later thwart all but the best-adapted of programmes. This historic paradox, which has intensified over the decades since Lukács wrote, with the widening of popular claims to entitlement and participation in public affairs, has done more than any local disappointment or scandal, however great in itself, to discredit the very idea of politics. But if politics as deliberative intervention in social relations as a whole is the supreme instance of 'general labour', it is not the only one. Culture, after all, is coextensive with social relations as a whole—and can, indeed, be represented, in specific cultural practices, such as that of Kulturkritik, as an alternative community of meanings and values.

---

28   Karl Marx, *Capital*, *Volume 1*, London 1976 [1869], pp. 635, 667.

For Herbert Marcuse, writing in the heroic phase of twentieth-century Kulturkritik, the modern ideal of culture functioned as a contemplative resolution of the objective disorder of bourgeois society.

Raymond Williams's *Culture and Society*, which, for all its differences of style and procedure, offers a congruent interpretation, traced the formation of culture as 'an abstraction and an absolute', as the last court of appeal.[29] Matthew Arnold, who was the pivotal figure in Williams's history, looked towards an ideal fusion of culture in that sense with its practical equivalent, the state. Metacultural discourse has been the form in which culture dissolves the political and takes up the general labour proper to it, assuming the role of a valid social authority.

However, the terms and agencies of that authority are not simply given. Culture, precisely because it is no less but also no more than the instance of meaning in social relations, is wholly implicated in all social antagonism, and, latterly, as 'the culture industry', in the ordinary conflicts of capitalist production itself. Intelligentsias, diverse in their provenance, occupational composition and social affinities, do not spontaneously give voice to a self-evident general interest. Even more so than politics, therefore, culture and intellectuals alike appear both central and marginal, commanding and merely pretentious, sublime and ridiculous, everything and nothing. Paul Valéry's satiric dream-vision has lost none of its sting:

> Tatters of dream came to me. I formed figures which I called 'Intellectuals'. Men almost motionless, who caused great movement in the world. Or very animated men, by the lively action of whose hands and mouths, imperceptible powers and essentially invisible objects were made manifest . . . Men of *thought*, Men of *letters*, Men of *science*, *Artists*—Causes, living causes, individuate causes, minimal causes, causes within causes and inexplicable to themselves—and causes whose effects were as vain, but at the same time as

---

29   Williams, *Culture and Society*, p. 17.

prodigiously important, *as I wished*. . . . The universe of these causes and their effects existed and did not exist. This system of strange acts, productions, and prodigies had the all-power-ful and vacant reality of a game of cards. Inspirations, medita-tions, works, glory, talents, it took no more than a certain look to make these things nearly everything, and a certain other look to reduce them to nearly nothing . . . [And among these intellectuals] the most ridiculous were those who made themselves, on their own authority, the judges and justices of the tribe.[30]

Such images of culture and intellectuals are stock items in every-day discourse, polite and popular, and with good historical cause. What Marx said of the quarrel between romantics and utilitarians applies equally to the vexatious problems of 'culture' and 'intel-lectuals': they are commonplaces in the spontaneous discourse of capitalist society, and will go on circulating 'up to its blessed end'.[31] Seeking always to manage the objective social contradic-tions that irritate it into life, metacultural discourse is constitu-tionally dependent on a rhetoric of 'splitting'. In a process akin to that described in the psychoanalytic tradition, the ambivalences and ambiguities of 'culture' and 'intellectuals' in a capitalist soci-ety are rewritten as fateful polarities of good and bad, true and false, high and low.[32] Kulturkritik offers the simpler illustration: 'culture' (good) must repeatedly discover 'civilization' (bad) and its approaching catastrophe, which is what confirms its own iden-tity and mission. Intellectuals must either conform to their moral essence or pervert it. They are either true *clercs* or treacherous accomplices of the market and the masses. Cultural Studies, a complex formation in which metacultural discourse is tendentially dominant but not necessarily so, presents a more variegated

---

30   Paul Valéry, *Monsieur Teste*, trans. J. Mathews, New York 1948, pp. 61–2.

31   Karl Marx, *Grundrisse: Foundations of the Critique of Political Economy (Rough Draft)*, trans. M. Nicolaus, Harmondsworth 1973, p. 162.

32   For lucid, scholarly accounts of Freud's 'splitting of the ego' and Melanie Klein's 'splitting of the object', see Jean Laplanche and Jean-Bertrand Pontalis, *The Language of Psychoanalysis*, trans. D. Nicholson-Smith, London 1988, pp. 427–30.

picture, but not a fundamentally different one. Would-be organic intellectuals, who may go so far as to renounce the title of intellectual for the common world of fans, must repeatedly discover the truth of popular culture, must always bear witness to it in defiance of the powers of 'culture with a capital C', which is also the left with a capital 'L'.

Metacultural discourse, it might be said, is a form of resistance through ritual, offering what the Birmingham circle would once have conceptualized as a 'magical solution' to the poverty of politics in bourgeois society. The difference between its older and more recent phases is one of temporality. Seen as Lukács saw it, the perverse autonomy of 'economics' in the capitalist mode of production is uncheckable. 'Conscious action directed towards the comprehended totality of society' is inconceivable except as revolution. 'Socialization' of production, its 'annulment' in the reified form of 'economics', is the structural condition of a collective life in which culture might really become the social dominant. And that outcome is contingent upon the mustering and exercise of effective political force in and against the historical present. Metacultural discourse elaborates the alternative, which itself assumes two forms. Kulturkritik looks to the past for the symbolic metapolitical forces capable of subduing civilized anarchy. Scrutiny's images of public virtue, of 'disinterested' governance of the whole, were feudal in provenance. Its critical meritocrats, like Mannheim's, would be a new priesthood. In Cultural Studies, the unquenched desire for an emancipated future has powered a symbolic transformation of the present. In the great commodity display of modern times, where Kulturkritik saw only indifference, standardization and levelling down, Cultural Studies prefers to see only use-values, sensuousness and a rainbow of discretionary potential. The fascination with 'youth' is telling. The slow reach has attained the speed of time travel. It can seem, on a good day, as if Lukács's vision has been realized, as if popular culture has outrun 'mere ideology' and the 'violence' of politics, to take final, unmediated possession of itself and its social world.

The authority that metacultural discourse recalls from the past promotes order and wholeness. The authority it alternatively borrows from the future affirms difference—and that not only as diversity, but as the heterogeneity that asserts itself within the normalizing frames of reason or humanity or nation, disrupting them. That contrast is historically substantial, as any comparative biographical survey of Kulturkritik and Cultural Studies would show. Yet, it has not been sufficient to rupture the formal continuity of metaculture, which, in either mode, invents an authoritative subject, 'good' culture, be it minority or popular, whose function is to mediate a symbolic metapolitical resolution of the contradictions of capitalist modernity. Popular culture, as it appears in this rarefied discursive construction, replays the dialectic of the high tradition that concerned Marcuse in the 1930s: it, too, is 'affirmative', in both the good and the bad senses. The excitable 'conformism' and 'populism' for which Cultural Studies has been chided run parallel to the negativism and elitism of Kulturkritik. They, too, are driven by an ambiguous 'promise of happiness'. Conformity here is not merely pragmatic adaptation to an overwhelming reality, even if it must always resemble that, but a deflated utopianism.

Cultural Politics?

Metacultural discourse is a creature of discrepancy, for which it constitutes itself as resolution. The discrepancy is that of culture and politics in the plane of social authority. In the earlier phase, that of Kulturkritik, the critique of politics is flat and final. Politics cannot metabolize the moral insights of culture, and is therefore inherently deficient as a social form. If not shunned altogether, as Benda preferred, it must be regulated by a superordinate politics of mind. Cultural Studies repudiates this tradition on demonstratively political grounds, but only to submit 'its own' polity, that of the left, to the same critique, with comparable effects. The progressive foregrounding of subjectivity in Cultural Studies and the privileging of identity as the site and stake of social antagonism achieve far more than the enrichment and complication they plausibly offer—or rather, much less than that—if, in theoretical reality, there is no longer a valid and specifically political practice to enrich or complicate. The problem that animates and seemingly justifies metacultural discourse, is not, at bottom, one of moral substance—having to do with specific social interests and purposes—however graphically the 'content' of politics may have featured in the record of critical controversy. It is one of form.

Only the typical dualism of Kulturkritik—the splitting of culture and civilization—obscures the insight on which Cultural Studies is founded. If culture, in its general reality, is the moment of meaning in social relations, if it is nothing less but also nothing more than the sense-making element of all practice, then it cannot also be exalted as the higher moral tribunal before which the lower claims of politics must submit to arbitration. On the contrary, and for the same reason, there is no instance of culture that is exempt from political implication. But the same sanction must then apply to popular culture, which, likewise, may not be privileged as Cultural Studies would wish. Moreover, to pass from that crucial founding insight to the commonplace that 'everything is political' is to scant the apparently contradictory · insight on which Kulturkritik drew for its compelling pejorative visions of modernity: politics is never everything. This seems paradoxical. After all, the specific practice of politics is to determine the totality of social relations in a given space. But this quintessentially general labour is specialized in mode. It is normally deliberative in character, governed by the question, What is to be *done*? Political utterance, then, is always injunctive, regardless of its medium, occasion or genre. It wills, urges, dictates. Its aim is to secure assent (a process in which issues of identity are indeed central) and, failing that, compliance, of which coercion furnishes the last guarantee. Cultural practices proper—those second-order elaborations of social meaning whose principal function is signification—have no need of that modal specialization, or no authoritative access to it, even where they pursue 'political' ends. They lack the formal distinction of political practice, from which they differ, correspondingly, in their norms of judgement. Culture may absolutize any value (including, as metaculture, that of itself). It may offer an infinity of moral discriminations, in mutually irreducible patterns. No meaning or value simply translates any other. Politics, whose rationale is to secure this or that general condition of existence, in a determinate social perspective, must always seek optimal terms of alignment, of solidarity and antagonism. Contrariwise, a political project may entail promoting division in a domain of cultural affinity, and for the same basic reason. Thus, as Gramsci perceived, political and cultural evaluation tend spontaneously towards non-coordination: each with respect to the other is both excessive (too broad, too narrow) and insufficient (too broad, too narrow).[33] The culture–politics discrepancy is always historically specific. It is the crisis of national tradition, or democratic legitimacy, or public standards, or class-consciousness, or ethnic continuity. Nevertheless, discrepancy itself is the general rule.

The rule is general, and also without discernible limit of jurisdiction, for if politics remains modally specialized even when conducted wholly in the plane of culture, then Lukács's vision of free and fluent human self-elaboration must be qualified. Even if cultural practice were to be released from 'mere ideology' and political practice from the necessity of 'violence', the discrepancy would persist into a future beyond lucid imagining. For just so long, Marcuse's 'affirmative culture' would continue in its equivocal elaboration of the promise of happiness, in a purely 'inward' cancellation of objective social contradictions, which would thereby be spared more consequential political attack. And so also, therefore, would metacultural discourse, which is the most general form of that affirmation, synoptic and engaged, embodying the will to resolution. Yet it does not follow necessarily that metaculture constitutes the inescapable discursive condition of critical thought, either in that elusive future or in the more tangible one we already inhabit. The only necessity in the case is that of discrepancy itself, which, once grasped as such, appears in another aspect, not as a place of historic frustration and wish-fulfilment but as a space of possibility.

'Cultural politics' is a spacious category. Socially committed art practice and criticism are a familiar instance. Stuart Hall's

---

33 Antonio Gramsci, *Selections from Cultural Writings*, ed. David Forgács and Geoffrey Nowell-Smith, London 1985, pp. 99–102.

explorations of new ethnicities and black popular culture exemplify this kind of cultural politics. Public policy is the ground of another kind, which controversies over national 'heritage' richly illustrate;[34] and in a development especially associated with Tony Bennett, this has assumed the form of 'cultural policy studies'.[35] Bennett's project is avowedly reformist, entailing a break from 'criticism' in favour of 'technical' intervention in institutions: 'Cultural studies might envisage its role as consisting of the training of cultural technicians.'[36] Glenn Jordan and Chris Weedon, in contrast, reaffirm the liberationist mission of the discipline. 'Cultural politics', they say, in their book of that name, 'is the struggle to fix meanings in the interest of particular groups.'[37]

> Whose culture shall be the official one and whose shall be subordinated? What cultures shall be regarded as worthy of display and which shall be hidden? Whose history shall be remembered and whose marginalized? What images of social life shall be projected and which shall be marginalized? What voices shall be heard and on what basis? This is the realm of cultural politics.[38]

These questions are unarguably fundamental. But there is a further question, not itself political, to put in return: is there any cultural practice that would not be politics, or any politics that would not be cultural? It seems not: *'everything* in social and cultural life is

---

34   Patrick Wright, *On Living in an Old Country: The National Past in Contemporary Britain*, London 1985; Raphael Samuel, *Theatres of Memory, Volume 1: Past and Present in Contemporary Culture*, London 1994.

35   Tony Bennett, 'Putting Policy into Cultural Studies', in Grossberg et al., *Cultural Studies*. For two dissenting judgements, see Ien Ang, 'Dismantling "Cultural Studies"?' and Tom O'Regan, '(Mis)taking Policy: Notes on the Cultural Policy Debate', both in *Cultural Studies*, vol. 6, no. 3, 1992. Compare Jim McGuigan, *Culture and the Public Sphere*, London 1996, p. 5, who distinguishes between 'cultural politics', to which he would refer Hall's arguments over black representation, and 'the politics of culture', which includes 'policy analysis and policy formulation'.

36   Tony Bennett, 'Useful Culture', in Blundell et al., *Relocating Cultural Studies*, p. 83.

37   Glenn Jordan and Chris Weedon, *Cultural Politics*, Oxford 1995, p. 544.

38   Typography modified. Ibid., p. 4.

fundamentally to do with *power*. It is integral to culture. *All signi-fying practices—that is, all practices that have meaning—involve relations of power'* (p. 11). The claim lodged here is more emphatic than precise, but its driving impulse seems unmistakable. 'Cultural politics', in a word, to which Jordan and Weedon resort more than once, is 'everything'. Their title is one word too long: the distinc-tion between culture and politics, on which their linkage logically depends, has been talked out of theoretical existence.

This need not happen. In the present context of argument, the idea of cultural politics acquires a precise conceptual value as a critical check on the metacultural dominant, and as the logical ground, though certainly not the substance, of an alternative. It has to be said again, with emphasis, that the analysis I propose here is formal in character, neither implying nor excluding any particular identification in the field of antagonistic social inter-ests—though, as I hope the analysis of metacultural discourse has helped to show, form is not a secondary matter. Cultural politics, as understood here, is not a special case of either politics or culture. Its field of action is mapped in the discrepancy between its constitutive terms, from which also it absorbs the tension that motivates it. Stuart Hall speaks too starkly, and perhaps with a certain romantic prejudice, in defining culture as 'infinite semio-sis', sense-making without end, and politics as its equally abstract regulator, 'arbitrary closure'.[39] Historical formations of culture, as structured social processes, are not so mercurial in their movement as either phrase suggests, and that definition of politics is already culturalist. Nevertheless, he exaggerates to the point. No politics, in so far as it respects its constitutive function, which is to deter-mine the order of social relations as a whole, can adequately repli-cate the contours and textures of the cultural formation in which it seeks to have effect. The field of identities, interests and values is always excessive. This excess has been simplified and spiritualized as the higher truth of humanity or the nation (Kulturkritik), and then simplified and politicized as the unregarded democracy of everyday life (Cultural Studies), but these alternative versions of

---

39   Hall, 'Culture and Power', p. 30.

the cultural principle are gambits in a space that does not answer to their reductive definitions. The excess has no fixed composition or tendency. It is a heterogeneous mass of possibilities old and new and never mutually translatable, possibilities no longer or not yet and perhaps never to be chartered as bearing general authority, as proper norms of political judgement. Culture is everything, in the sense that there is no social life outside formations of meaning, but it never adds up. Political practice seeks to determine social relations as a whole—a whole more richly differentiated than the subtlest of programmes, which, therefore, can never lucidly aspire to be everything. And in that necessary non-identity lies the very possibility of the activities, the interests, the perspectives that can meaningfully be distinguished as cultural politics.

Stuart Hall has emphasized the 'necessary modesty' of Cultural Studies. The point of these closing pages on the concept of cultural politics is to suggest that the immodesty his project-discipline has learnt willy-nilly from its authoritarian forebear, Kulturkritik, is, in theory at least, not necessary. Genealogy is not destiny. The social desire that metaculture encodes is inextinguishable: what compels it is Herder's 'image of happiness'. But metaculture as a discursive form is romance, a journey through the waste land in search of lost virtue or into an enchanted forest of commodities, where even the future is in season all year round. It is better, surely, to settle for lucidity—to honour the image of happiness 'negatively', as Adorno put it, by retaining the contradictions 'pure and uncompromised'[40]—and to enter cultural politics with a greater modesty that in fact subserves a greater ambition, as the art of the possible.

---

40   Theodor W. Adorno, *Prisms: Cultural Criticism and Society*, Cambridge, MA, 1981 [1955], p. 32.

2

STEFAN COLLINI

Culture Talk

The semantic field encompassed by the single term 'culture' is now so large and so complex, and possessed of such a tangled history, that it may no longer be really practicable to attempt to treat it as a single topic. The very existence of the plural, 'cultures', signifies a radically different subject-matter from that designated by what some, often defensively, always self-consciously, call 'culture with a capital C'. The adjectival forms throw further fat on the fire: the business of a cultural attaché may have nothing in common with that of a professor of Cultural Studies; 'cultural criticism' as practised by a descendant of the Frankfurt School will bear little resemblance to that carried out by a broadsheet theatre-reviewer. Any new book on the topic, even one clearly signalling its affiliation to one established academic discipline or discourse, has thus to pick its way very carefully through a minefield of potential misapprehensions.

'There are few easier paths into difficulty than the one paved with fixed expectations.' Thus Francis Mulhern, warning readers of *Culture/Metaculture* about what *not* to expect from it. But the warning could be repeated in a much more affirmative and annunciatory register. This slim, pocket-format volume comes disguised as a contribution to the 'New Critical Idiom' series, a collection clearly aimed at the floundering student and offering (in the words of the series blurb) to provide 'a handy, explanatory guide to the use (and abuse)' of the main elements in 'today's critical terminology'. But there is little, its physical shape apart, that is 'handy' about this short book, which is far removed indeed from those warmed-over summaries of other people's ideas that now flood this particular market. For *Culture/Metaculture* is an important theoretical statement in its own right; with its publication, Mulhern may well have taken a step towards becoming one of those authors whose ideas will be summarized in the next generation of 'handy guides'.

The book will no doubt provoke disagreement from more or less all quarters (I have my two pennyworth to throw in presently), but it should first be said in plainest terms that this is in many ways a brilliant work. There has long been a distinctive economy and conceptual neatness about Mulhern's writing, but here these qualities mutate, as it were, into a more confident version of themselves, producing an impressive analytic power and incisiveness of phrase, especially in the highly condensed closing pages. The book is, then, not exactly a wolf in sheep's clothing, but rather a kind of stylish heist in which unsuspecting readers are first enticed in by a familiar-looking array of usual suspects (from Mannheim and Leavis on to Williams, Hall and company), and then are systematically stripped of all their accumulated assumptions about 'culture and society', before being released into an austere, somewhat impenetrable space of 'cultural politics', a bracing but not at all reassuring space where so much of what one might have thought had been done once and for all now appears, in the chill half-light cast by Mulhern's unforgiving analysis, to need doing all over again. In fact, there is a slightly Beckettian feel about the ending: try again, fail again, fail better. Or, adapting another idiom close to home for Mulhern: strenuousness of the intellect, stoicism of the will.

It is correspondingly difficult to summarize the contents of this dense, challenging little book. Mulhern's central argument is that although the tradition which he calls 'Kulturkritik' (of which more in a moment) and the movement or discipline now called 'Cultural Studies' may appear to be almost diametrically opposed in their aims and political affiliations, they in fact exhibit a fundamental continuity at the level of form. They each appeal to a (very different) notion of 'culture' to 'mediate a symbolic metapolitical resolution of the contradictions of capitalist modernity'. 'Kulturkritik' attempts to 'spiritualize' the notion as 'the higher truth of humanity or the nation'; Cultural Studies attempts to 'politicize' it as 'the unregarded democracy of everyday life'. These kinds of explicit appeal to 'culture' Mulhern christens 'metacultural discourse', that is, 'discourse in which culture addresses its own generality and conditions of existence'. But metacultural discourse, he urges, should not deceive itself that it can somehow supplant the authority of politics, and in place of such hubristic practices, he recommends a more modestly framed conception of 'cultural politics'.

In practical terms, the first part of the book contains brief discussions of Mann, Benda, Ortega, Leavis and Mannheim; of Freud, Woolf and Orwell, of Eliot and Hoggart; and then a much longer account of Raymond Williams. The second part takes up Williams (again) and the Birmingham Centre for Contemporary Cultural Studies, deals at some length with Stuart Hall, and then touches on the work of several recent practitioners of Cultural Studies. The brief concluding section states his own alternative position. It should be recorded that several paragraphs in this book have done more than one tour of duty before. Thus, much the greater part of the chapters on Hoggart and Williams is reproduced verbatim from the essay 'A Welfare Culture? Hoggart and Williams in the Fifties', which first appeared in *Radical Philosophy* in 1996 and was then republished in Mulhern's collection *The Present Lasts a Long Time: Essays in Cultural Politics* (1999). Similarly, his account of Benda, Mannheim and company borrows from other essays reprinted in that volume—the earliest of which was first published as far back as 1981—while Leavis has, of course, been at the heart of Mulhern's critical concerns from the very outset of his career. It is in the more extended account of Cultural Studies, and especially in the argument about the hidden continuity of form between that discipline and the Kulturkritik tradition, that the novelty of the book is chiefly to be found.

Birmingham and Beyond

Mulhern says several times (in slightly differing terms) that the defining aim of Cultural Studies has been 'to de-mystify the presumptive authority of Kulturkritik', that as a movement (which in some ways describes it better than 'discipline') its informing aspiration has been to contest the status of the kind of 'culture' laid claim to by the older tradition. He emphasizes that 'popular creativity' is 'the very principle of Cultural Studies', and points to the pitfalls of treating some selection of such activities as a locus of value. He is properly severe on the posturing of 'the intellectual as fan' and devastating on the 'street pastoral' of certain theorists' invocation of an implausibly unmediated set of 'spontaneous' popular tastes. Following other critics, he dissects the desire in Cultural Studies to '*be* politics', to constantly assert that what one is doing is, somehow, political, indeed more 'political' than conventional politics. And he approvingly cites Todd Gitlin's call for a 'harder-headed, less wishful cultural studies, free of the burden of imagining itself to be a political practice'. Mulhern writes (as some other critics, including myself, clearly do not) from a position that is in some ways *inside* contemporary Cultural Studies—one which, as always, gives his critique more purchase and more force. But although deeply familiar with this literature, he maintains a certain theoretical distance from its populist enthusiasms, and his own idiom is inflected by the austerer tones derived from the European high Marxist tradition of Gramsci, Lukács and Adorno.

It is clear that the two figures who most engage Mulhern's intellectual energies in this book are Williams and Hall. No other writers mentioned in the book are discussed at anything like the same length nor, despite occasional polite remarks, with the same respect—a respect which expresses itself in the form of that highest tribute, extended and responsible criticism. The section on Hall is particularly impressive, involving a neat exercise in practical criticism (if Mulhern will forgive the term) on Hall's style, especially the function of its characteristic 'thickness of modification'. These tics, Mulhern acutely observes, give the appearance of exactness without the reality. 'Emphasis, in cases such as these, is the opposite of what it purports to be: it is a way of not coming to the point. It is the deceptive figure of theoretical evasion.' His analysis here is theoretically as well as stylistically sharp, indicating, for example, the loss of explanatory power in Hall's tendency to treat 'the conjunctural' and 'the concrete' as equivalents. (I have to say that the picture of Hall which emerges from Mulhern's analysis, though it is no part of the latter's intention so to represent him, seems to me that of an exceptionally alert and responsive social critic who cannot quite bring himself to acknowledge that his most fruitful perceptions are constantly escaping, and thereby drawing attention to, the limits of his inherited materialist idiom.)

I have two reservations about the argument of the book, reservations which, though fundamental, do not seem to me to detract from its value but, rather, to challenge its self-description. The first concerns his construction of the tradition of 'Kulturkritik', while the second focuses on his analysis of the function of the idea of 'culture' itself and the role of his own book in relation to this.

It is vitally important, I believe, to recognize that 'Kulturkritik', as the term is used in this book, designates a position or tradition that has been constructed by Mulhern himself. Of course, in its original German it refers to a recognizable genre that stretches back, perhaps, as far as the end of the eighteenth century. But Mulhern uses the term to refer to something both more general and more specific than that particular German tradition. It is more general because for him it is Europe-wide, embracing figures as different as Benda and Leavis as well as those like Mann who undeniably belong under the heading as conventionally used. But it is also more specific, partly because for Mulhern it effectively begins in 1918 (and flourishes most notably between the wars, albeit with post-war British continuations), but partly because it denotes a particular intellectual and political conjunction. 'Kulturkritik', as used here, designates the revulsion from 'mass society' of a mandarin elite, the appeal to an inherited, if also largely intangible, way of life or 'national spirit', most lastingly embodied in the higher artistic forms, which is seen as threatened by democracy and the popularization of taste. The polarity between 'minority culture' and 'mass civilization' is constitutive of the critical position occupied by this tradition.

A Truncated Tradition

Now, no one could deny that something like this was a powerful strain in twentieth-century European social thought, but, first, the figures whom Mulhern cites as its representatives seem a heterogeneous crew, exhibiting more disparities than resemblances; and, second, the 'tradition' so constructed is far from coextensive with all invocations of the critical value of 'culture'. Thus Benda, for example, surely belongs in a specifically French tradition of looking to a transcendent conception of Reason to function as a *pouvoir spirituel*, not only dismissive of all engagement with mere practice but, more particularly, explicitly hostile to that Germanic insistence on the priority of a *national* way of life that was such a feature of the core tradition of Kulturkritik (even though Benda himself was not above treating France as the national home of the universal). By starting his account of the tradition in 1918, Mulhern makes European inter-war cultural pessimism its defining moment, so that the appeal to 'culture' has to be socially elitist, culturally alarmist and politically conservative. But this foreshortens and radically distorts the historical possibilities. If one returned to, say, Ruskin and Morris, or even, in the period Mulhern focuses on, to Tawney, one would find a tradition of social criticism that in various ways appeals to what it understands by 'culture' and yet displays few of the reactionary features Mulhern makes constitutive of 'Kulturkritik'.

The structure of Mulhern's argument assigns 'Kulturkritik' firmly to the past, not just chronologically by tying it to the first half of the twentieth century, but also in the sense of treating it as a wholly discredited enterprise. It is upon this opening move that the logic of his book depends. What, from there, he goes on to say about a certain structural or formal continuity between this alleged tradition and Cultural Studies seems to me wholly persuasive and valuable. But what it rules out, at a stroke, is the validity of any attempt to speak from 'culture' as part of political debate within society. To seek to draw upon a source of critical thinking which may help contest some of the exploitative effects of instrumental reason in contemporary global politics is not simply to repeat some outmoded mandarin gesture. One may acknowledge the force of Williams's criticisms of the 'culture and society tradition', and indeed profit from Mulhern's own detailed criticism of his predecessors, while at the same time still finding 'culture' a useful mnemonic for the kinds of values that those principally engaged in controlling the wealth and power of the world habitually tend to neglect. Seen in this way, 'culture' still names an ethical move, an allusion to the bearing which that kind of disinterested or auto-telic exploration of human possibility, characteristically (but not exclusively) pursued in artistic and intellectual activity, can have upon those processes that are governed by the need to bring about proximate instrumental ends.

This leads into my second reservation. It is not clear to me that Mulhern's own book is exempt from the charges he lays against what he calls 'metacultural discourse', but, by the same token, I do not necessarily see this as a bad thing (this is what I meant by saying that I am challenging the book's self-description rather than its value).

As I have said, Mulhern describes the alternative practice he wishes to recommend as 'cultural politics', in a very specific and idiosyncratic sense of that term. Culture and politics will, he asserts, always be 'discrepant', and this discrepancy should be seen not just as a negative or awkward case of non-correspondence, 'but as a space of possibility'. 'Cultural politics', then, seems to entail a constant acknowledgement of this 'discrepancy', an acknowledge-ment which would prevent us succumbing to the defining illusion of metacultural discourse (that an essentialized, largely inherited 'culture' provides some kind of overarching or corrective locus of value and hence of authority), but which would still seem to furnish us with grounds from which to criticize any actual politics. For no actual politics can be, as it were, adequate—Arnoldian vocabulary has a way of seeping back in—to the cultural complexity of the social setting in which it seeks to operate. (This is offered as a conceptual truth, not as an empirical judgement on the limitations of actually existing politicians.) The 'excess' should not, however, be reduced to 'the higher truth of humanity', as 'Kulturkritik' was wont to do; nor, as Cultural Studies is wont to do, to 'the unregarded democracy of everyday life'. What he here calls 'the cultural principle' is not, in those ways, fixed in its content. Between, on the one hand, the necessary failure of 'politics' to encompass the complexity of the meaning-bearing reality within which it seeks to act, and, on the other hand, the necessarily 'heterogeneous mass of possibilities' which can never be codified into a determinate body of works or activities designated 'culture', lies the possibility of 'cultural politics'.

'Art of the Possible'

It is, in the end, clearer what the ethos of Mulhern's 'cultural politics' is supposed to be—modest, unillusioned, accepting of irresolvable antinomies—than what, as an activity, it actually amounts to. Stripped of its strenuous refusal of all comforting self-justifications, his 'cultural politics' may at first appear hard to distinguish from what others might simply call 'politics', a thought reinforced by the fact that the very final phrase of the book speaks of understanding cultural politics as 'the art of the possible'. This phrase, beloved of pragmatic and generally conservative politicians (R. A. Butler used it for the title of his autobiography), closes the book with a disconcerting bump. In itself, the use of the phrase might seem to signal the abandonment of the ambition of critique, which would be a very odd conclusion for a left cultural theorist to recommend. Mulhern is not, plainly, recommending this, though a chastened sense of the intractability of these issues does express itself in a (to my mind admirable) modesty of tone. But if 'cultural politics' is not just everyday politics by another name, if it somehow involves the field of 'culture' (as the whole conception of the book suggests it does), then it becomes important to see what the relation is between this distinctive sense of 'cultural politics' and what he characterizes as 'metacultural discourse'.

In the closing pages of the book, he concisely restates a central element of his argument: 'If culture, in its general reality, is the moment of meaning in social relations, if it is nothing less but also nothing more than the sense-making element of all practice, then it cannot also be exalted as the higher moral tribunal before which the lower claims of politics must submit to arbitration.' This is an excellent summary of the line of criticism that has flowed from the work of Williams and, to some extent, of Hall. However, the problem then is to ask whether there is any consequential distinction to be made between 'culture' and 'politics', if 'all practice', as is now sometimes urged, is to be seen as inherently political. Mulhern argues that politics is not, and cannot be, 'everything'. Politics he chooses to see as distinguished by its form, which will always be injunctive: the attempt to bring about a state of affairs on a collective social scale. But not all human activities have to have this form and, elaborating this point, he goes on to say: 'Cultural practices proper—those second-order elaborations of social meaning whose principal function is signification—have no need of that modal specialization.' However fruitful the general argument about the distinctive form of political activity may be, the bracketed phrase here sounds awfully like our old friend 'culture': not, to be sure, 'high culture' in its purely contingent social form (galleries, opera houses, and so on), but nonetheless those forms of signifying activity which are not principally governed by an instrumental purpose, let alone intent upon bringing about, amid the clash of contending interests, the least bad state of affairs in the world.

Mulhern says more than once that the 'fixed impulse' of metacultural discourse is 'to displace politics as a form of social authority'. This has an initial plausibility as a formulation on account of the primarily German antecedents of 'Kulturkritik', where Kultur did at times function in this way. But on a broader view, 'displace' surely seems too strong, and hence distorting: the impulse of self-conscious appeals to culture has rather been to introduce and make effective *in* public discussion the kinds of considerations that the instrumental and present-driven world of purely political discourse habitually underplays or neglects. But that being so, what Mulhern calls 'metacultural discourse' cannot be equated with 'Kulturkritik' (as he constitutes the tradition he so names) and Cultural Studies. Both of these traditions are only examples of the deployment of the standpoint of 'culture'; they are not exhaustive of its possibilities. Moreover, they are individual historical instances, as well as antitypes. Their particular *content*—a class-specific form of lost Eden on the one hand, a no less class-specific form of popular, democratic energy on the other—is indeed not simply to be endorsed as an adequate ground from which to challenge the everyday forms of contemporary politics. But that only underlines that we need to go further and recognize that what he calls 'metacultural discourse' is in fact the practice of reflexivity where the object of first-order discourse is society itself. In other words, it does not require the positing of 'culture' as some kind of given or transcendent locus of value; it only requires the presumption that disciplined reflection partly grounded in an extensive intellectual and aesthetic inheritance can furnish a place to stand in attempting to engage critically with the narrow pragmatism (or 'specialism') of any particular political programme. Mulhern's own politics, not to mention his conceptual sophistication, certainly mark a decisive distance from those he brackets as exponents of 'Kulturkritik'; but is there not a sense in which, in his own re-worked vocabulary, he is repeating precisely what he has earlier identified as the disabling gesture of all such criticism, namely the appeal to certain 'elaborations of social meaning whose principal function is signification', or, in other words, the appeal to culture?

Collective Reflections

It may be helpful here to return to some of the formulations in Williams's *Culture and Society*. Several of the glosses Williams gives on the term 'culture' involve a central emphasis on looking at 'the whole form of our common life', on 'the effort at total qualitative assessment'. I would argue that the *generality* of the perspective is the key here. The contrast is with all partial or specialized perspectives. Implicit in this (though not, perhaps, recognized in these terms by Williams himself) is the perception that instrumentality or practice can be seen as yet another form of specialization. 'Culture' is one of the shorthand terms for the 'standing back' or 'taking a more general view' which is the characteristic of intellectual labour in its broadest aspect. Part of what was *historically* misleading about the way Williams pursued this perception in

Culture and Society was that he equated earlier efforts to elaborate such a perspective with a critique of 'the bourgeois idea of society' (or 'individualism', as he also termed it), that is, in its positive form, with the working-class ethic of solidarity. This produced an oddly distorted picture of nineteenth-century British intellectual history, in which a wide range of writers and critics were recruited to speak for 'culture', leaving only a few implausibly strict political economists to serve as representatives of the 'society' side of his pairing.

But if, instead of following Williams in using this particular political contrast to organize our account of nineteenth- and early twentieth-century thought, we develop his perception that 'culture' came to stand for various attempts at 'total qualitative assessment', we shall find that *Culture/Metaculture* is more continuous with the traditions it criticizes than its self-description would have us believe. After all, in so far as the book is offering something other, or more, than 'politics', it surely depends upon the critical potential of that 'heterogeneous mass of possibilities' identified earlier. The critical function of the 'discrepancy' is what his own metacultural discourse seeks to establish. But does this then not bear a structural resemblance to 'the appeal to culture' characteristic of the earlier traditions? Is it not an attempt to do something more than merely endorse the norms of current political practice and discussion, precisely by identifying a level of considerations which might in some sense check or chastise any more restricted or near-sighted forms of political debate? Looked at in this way, Mulhern's argument does not escape the logic of metacultural discourse that he so brilliantly diagnoses: in other words, *discourse about metacultural discourse is still a form of metacultural discourse*. It is still trying to bring something to those forms of political discussion that operate with shorter horizons. And one of the uses of the protean term 'culture' is precisely to name the standpoint from which such criticism speaks—even such self-scrutinizing and theoretically acute criticism as Mulhern's. In other words, 'cultural politics', as Mulhern (sketchily) characterizes it, is bound to share the formal properties he identifies in appeals to 'culture' itself, but I would argue that this is in itself no bad thing. For it concerns nothing less than the bearing of intellectual and imaginative labour on those (other) aspects of the world that are principally determined by instrumental labour. Looked at in this way, what Mulhern calls 'cultural politics' seems to me to be one further formulation of the standpoint from which the task of aiming at 'total qualitative assessment' may be attempted; it is not the supersession of that task.

And this is the common ground of my two reservations. If you first reduce the various forms of the appeal to 'culture' to the narrow frame of 'Kulturkritik', then it becomes necessary to propose jettisoning this as always enacting an appeal to a lost Eden, a form of social virtue which actually expresses an elitist disdain for ordinary life. But if culture is seen as a useful shorthand for a set of collectively practised prompts to reflection—in other words, culture as the aspect of meaningfulness in all activities *raised to reflexivity*—then we should not simply disown these (and other) predecessors, however much we may wish to distance ourselves from the historically contingent content of their critiques. Mulhern himself, after all, is not in fact here practising 'the art of the possible': he is writing a book attempting to give a clearer analytical account of what can be involved in so doing. That is, properly in my view, the work of intellectuals (in one sense of that no less protean term). But it is not a *resolution* of the tensions between 'culture' and 'politics'; it is a further, cultural, *statement about* the relations between the two. It is, as I have tried to bring out, a very valuable and at times scintillating statement, but we should not lose sight of the fact that it is also recognizably a modern meditation upon (if Mulhern will forgive another antique formula) 'the function of criticism'.

II

3

FRANCIS MULHERN

Beyond Metaculture

The saying that texts are never finished, merely abandoned, is old but not toothless. It can bite, as I had cause to reflect in 'abandoning' *Culture/Metaculture*, some three years ago, not wholly reconciled. I am particularly grateful, then, for the critical responses it has attracted, and in the first place to Stefan Collini for 'Culture Talk'. Collini is an intellectual historian deeply versed in the politically assorted series of thinkers often dubbed 'the *Culture and Society* tradition'—in his own terms, the 'public moralists' of nineteenth- and twentieth-century Britain.[1] At the same time, he is probably still better known as a writer in that tradition, committed to the practice of 'the higher journalism', a non-specialist discourse engaging the general interests of a mixed readership.[2] This is the ground from which he approaches *Metaculture*. His discussion is generous beyond ordinary expectation, and at times unnerving in its empathetic reach. But above all, it sets out some fundamental objections, to which I wish to respond now, in an attempt to clarify and develop the sense of a position beyond metaculture.

'Metaculture' names a modern discursive formation in which 'culture', however understood, speaks of its own generality and historical conditions of existence. Its inherent strategic

---

1 Stefan Collini, *Public Moralists: Political Thought and Intellectual Life in Britain 1850–1930*, Oxford 1991.
2 Stefan Collini, *English Pasts: Essays in History and Culture*, Oxford 1999. See especially pp. 1–5 and 305–25.

impulse—failing which it would be no more than descriptive anthropology—is to mobilize 'culture' as a principle against the prevailing generality of 'politics' in the disputed plane of social authority. What speaks in metacultural discourse is the cultural principle itself, as it strives to dissolve the political as locus of general arbitration in social relations. Kulturkritik and Cultural Studies, typically contrasting in social attachment yet sharing this discursive template, have been strong versions of this metacultural will to authority. For the left, such logic is either inimical or self-defeating. The alternative begins with the theoretical recognition that cultural and political practice are structurally distinct, yielding mutually irreducible norms of judgement. Discrepancy is the necessary term of their relationship—and not a sign of blockage but a condition of practical possibility. Here, in a few sentences, are the core theses of *Metaculture*. As stated there, they have drawn criticism on both historical and theoretical grounds—and also fostered certain misunderstandings, for which I have to accept some responsibility. Collini's historical charge concerns my unorthodox deployment of the Germanic category of Kulturkritik.[3]

I. The Accents of Kulturkritik

Kulturkritik as it figures in *Metaculture* is my own 'construction', Collini warns, and a tendentious one. It is chronologically more limited than the historic genre whose common name it has been, reaching back no further than 1918, and geographically far wider, extending beyond the German-language zone to assemble 'a heterogeneous crew' of intellectuals from Spain, England and France— Mann, Mannheim and the later Freud, but also Ortega, Leavis and even Benda. Thus, designedly or not, 'European inter-war cultural pessimism' becomes 'the defining moment' of an actually diverse 'tradition', and 'the appeal to "culture" has to be socially elitist, culturally alarmist and politically conservative'—intrinsically, an

---

3   Deliberately rendered in this way, without italics or quotation marks.

intellectual trope of the right.[4] I wear my heart on my sleeve, it seems.

Of course, 'Kulturkritik' is a construction, just like 'absolutism', say, or 'modernism'. Construction and reconstruction are the process of all thought, as it labours to know reality. The pertinent critical question concerns the nature of the construction and its claim to rational plausibility. Generically viewed, *Metaculture* is an essay in the historical morphology of discourse. Its critical point of entry is *form*: the recurrence of certain relations among concepts (culture, politics, authority), a certain array of topoi (modernity as disintegration, for example), a certain ethos of address (the prophetic intellectual and kindred personae). The purpose of the analysis is to demonstrate the unity of its historical material at that specified level, to show that this 'heterogeneous crew', for all their acknowledged differences of national and disciplinary sensibility, political leaning and intellectual personality, acted within a shared discursive order and subserved its governing logic. Collini is on the whole gratifyingly clear about the 'structural or formal' priorities of the analysis, even declaring himself persuaded by the account of the relations between Kulturkritik and Cultural Studies. But here, momentarily, he responds as if to another kind of work.

A more spacious, more richly historical book would range more widely. It would register other national varieties from the same period—Huizinga's *The Shadow of the Future* and the Russian *Vekhi*, for example—and might probe the significance of a thinker such as Croce, whose thought has some formal affinity with Kulturkritik, but perhaps no more substantial association. Even if not venturing beyond the borders of Europe, it would at least acknowledge the presence of Kulturkritik, in derived or parallel forms, in other continents. A more strongly comparative study would not merely record the manifest international variations in the discourse, but would attempt to make historical sense of them. Thus, Leavis differed most clearly from his European counterparts in the priority he accorded to the economic over the political

---

4   'Culture Talk', above, p. 36.

dimension of modernity. Conjunctural and more enduring conditions alike contributed to this distribution. Mann wrote in the last days of Wilhelmine Germany, Mannheim in the later years of Weimar. Ortega's manifesto coincided with the birth of republican Spain. Benda's formative public engagement was as a Dreyfusard; decades later, he joined the mobilization against the Croix de Feu. In Britain, on the other hand, with a constitutional matrix long settled and largely exempt from political controversy, there was nothing to distract attention from the latest novelties in a continuing process of economic transformation: Fordism and the culture industry, not the new politics of labour, are the privileged omens in Leavis's symptomatology.

In this way, the variegated Kulturkritik of the 1920s observed the geographical pattern set by Hobsbawm's 'dual revolution', but with effects that cannot be appraised by a simple reckoning of similarities versus differences. Readers of *Scrutiny* were as much aware of Martin Turnell's 'French' critique of democracy as of Leavis's better-known extension of the 'English' critique of industrialism. Collini is a little too taken with Benda's rationalism and cosmopolitanism—which reached its limits at the Franco-German border.[5] His glassy abstractions are perhaps not in the English manner, but his tendency, which Collini admits, to 'treat France as the national home of the universal' has a strict counterpart in Leavis's imaginary England. The favouring condition of these bewitching identifications was in both cases political. Leavis's national humanism, his fluent elision of Englishness and 'life' *tout court*, depended for its intuitive plausibility on the inherited reality of a world empire; Benda's universalism was rooted in the abstract codes of the Third Republic. For Mann, in contrast, the universal was a spurious, alien—'Roman'—value: in this sense, he had no equivalent vision of Germany. Writing as subject of a failed empire, bracing himself for the advent of a civic equality he thought second best, he spoke for a cherished particularism, an

---

5   *La Trahison des clercs* is remembered for its chaste intellectualism, but not for its renewed insistence that the Central Powers alone bore the responsibility for the First World War.

introverted *Sonderweg* of the spirit. Thus, his nationalism was, in context and propensity, a true negative of the others. Three images of cultural distinction, marked and contrasted, or even opposed, in national terms, all claiming moral precedence over the modern political order, each one a sublimation of given political conditions.

Varieties of Political Invariance

So far at least, then, consideration of the national diversity of Kulturkritik yields evidence for, not against, its discursive unity. The cases of Mannheim and Ortega, whose national identifications were complicated by the circumstances of exile and education respectively, might prove less amenable in this respect. More important, as clearly contrasted liberals of the left and right, they forestall any claim that Kulturkritik was uniformly 'conservative' or 'reactionary'. That is not the claim of *Metaculture*, nor do the arguments of the book presuppose it—fortunately, since the alternative would have been shipwreck. Kulturkritik was and remains politically changeable, in its simpler forms and still more in its alloyed varieties. Benda, when he felt himself 'permitted' to intervene, did so on the side of the left, not even straining at a manifesto with the word 'revolutionary' in its banner. Mann soon endorsed the Weimar constitution, and later put his eminence at the service of intellectual anti-fascism. Ortega responded differently, quitting Spain for Argentina at the outbreak of the Civil War. *Scrutiny*'s collaborators included a socialist like L. C. Knights and a clerico-rightist like Turnell, as well as their elusively liberal chief editor—Leavis, who in the tricky currents of the 1930s held the journal to the left, only later turning visibly rightwards. Discursive hybrids call for a particular effort of discrimination. *A Room of One's Own* is rendered incoherent by the internalized pressure of Bloomsbury's presumptuous, rentier version of Kulturkritik, but to say this is not to disallow Woolf's left-wing sympathies or cancel the feminism of her book (or, as I neglected to add, of the distinct and later *Three Guineas*). Other hybrids are simpler. Richard Hoggart has substantiated the possibility of a

stable, enduring Kulturkritik of the left, social-democratic conviction adapting Leavisian diagnostics to assert the value of diffusion
as progress, the quickening of popular life by culture broadly cast.
Collini feels much closer to that work than I do (and has a correspondingly much lower opinion of Raymond Williams, whose
cultural politics are fundamentally distinct).[6] But the suggestion—to which the logic of his charge commits him—that my
general categories cannot properly accommodate that work, even
as historical possibility, is unconvincing. As *Metaculture* puts it, in
terms that mark a political distance but hardly suppress the historical distinction: 'In Richard Hoggart, the British labour movement
found its own Matthew Arnold.'

The political habitus of Kulturkritik is of another order:
conservative, liberal or socialist, this discourse thrives on *climacterics*, and its recurring tendency is *authoritarian*. The canonical
texts inscribe the climacteric in their forms, which more or less
closely resemble the manifesto—the general alert, the recall to
duty, the theses nailed to the bookshop door. Kulturkritik is 'occa-
sionalist' in the sense that word acquires in Carl Schmitt's critique
of political romanticism.[7] Its relation to the pre-given terms of
political engagement is subject to 'a higher third', which reframes
politics as such as a constituent of the crisis, not the dimension in

---

6   See Collini, 'Critical Minds: Raymond Williams and Richard Hoggart', in
English Pasts, pp. 210–30. The difference was already formulated in the conclusion
of Williams's *Culture and Society*. Collini cites this text in familiar, questionable
terms, speaking of its 'equation' of the 'cultural' critique of bourgeois individualism
with 'the working-class ethic of solidarity' (p. 51). In fact, as I read it, Williams
posits not two but three 'ideas of the nature of social relationship', and the third is
'the reforming bourgeois modification' of individualism, or 'the idea of service'.
This idea, which has predominated 'from Coleridge to Tawney', is distinct from the
ethic of solidarity, and 'in practice' stands 'opposed' to it (*Culture and Society*,
Harmondsworth 1961, pp. 312–13, 315). Hoggart showed, in his own career, that
individual hybrids of solidarity and service were indeed possible, if only within the
strategic horizons of Labourism and the BBC. The critique of that reforming
paternalism was, for Williams, the prelude to an alternative, socialist and democratic,
theory and politics of cultural practice and organization.

7   Carl Schmitt, *Political Romanticism*, Cambridge, MA, and London 1986
[1919]. Written in 1917–18, this work is almost exactly contemporaneous with
Mann's *Reflections of an Unpolitical Man*.

which it may be dealt with. Politics stands exposed as the modern pretender to social authority, whose legitimate form (past and, as it may be, prospective) is the cultural principle. That superordination of culture-as-principle, and of an intellectual corps privy to its meanings, can only be authoritarian, in final effect, even where the associated social aspiration is benign and progressive. There are residues of this in Hoggart's *Uses of Literacy*, and far more substantial deposits in the writings of R. H. Tawney, whom Collini cites as one index of the historical complication he misses in *Metaculture*. A Christian socialist and inspiration to generations of thoughtful Labour supporters, Tawney cannot be denied his place in the intellectual history of the British left. Yet his critique of 'the acquisitive society', set out in the book of that name, was driven by idealized memories of pre-industrial England and issued in a strategy appealing to the supreme moral authority of a rearmed national Church. The homology with Kulturkritik is manifest, as Collini would surely agree: the critical account I have just summarized is his own.[8]

II. A Marxist Kulturkritik?

There remains an oddity in the expanded–restricted concept of Kulturkritik. If the chronological foreshortening of my discussion is regrettable, it is not because of any attendant foreclosure of political possibilities. It is because a longer historical retrospect would have emphasized the genealogical specificity of Kulturkritik as a descendant of German and English Romanticism. A few introductory paragraphs on Herder and Arnold were the belated token acknowledgement of this—like most 'introductions', written last, without real power to modify the substantive text. Had things gone otherwise, I still might not have said much more about the nineteenth century; but the representation of mid-twentieth-century German thought would certainly have been different. Martin Ryle has expressed 'surprise' at the absence of 'any

---

8   Collini, 'Moral Mind: R. H. Tawney', in *English Pasts*, pp. 177–94.

systematic account of the Frankfurt School'; Peter Osborne finds the omission 'unfortunate'.[9] They have reason. Marcuse and Adorno feature in *Metaculture* as mentors in my own cause, deracinated subjects of a certain theoretical position, but not more concretely, as what they historically were: critical intellectuals formed in strong German traditions. Failing to register this, the book spared itself reflection on the disconcerting possibility it appeared to exclude in advance, that of a Marxist Kulturkritik.

The 'culture' of which Marcuse spoke in his classic 1937 study was not Mann's *Kultur*.[10] Universal in principle, rather than national, it was his critical reconstruction of the status and function assigned to literature and the arts in a bourgeois society. Culture in this sense is the negation of a social order for which, in the same gesture, it composes a transfiguring alibi. Committed to the possibilities of wholeness and resolution in human affairs ('the pacification of existence', as Marcuse would later say), yet actualizing them only in the abstracted, inward life of sensibility, culture honours the promise of happiness but only, so to speak, as a matter of form. A bad utopia, it 'affirms' in social practice what, as imagination, it calls to account. Sensibility, the faculty that gives access to cultural experience and grows subtle in those who exercise it, is the mode in which unfree subjects choose between inconsolable quietism and a good conscience.[11]

For Marcuse, this 'culture' signified the place of art and literature in capitalist social relations. Its discursive authority was an index of oppression, not a resource for an emancipated future. Dismissing Karl Kautsky's adumbration of 'the "coming happiness"', he projected an alternative vision of social transformation: not the mass 'conquest' of culture but its 'elimination'.[12] Adorno,

---

9   Martin Ryle, 'Tempting Relevancies', *Radical Philosophy* 103, September–October 2000, p. 46; Peter Osborne, *Philosophy in Cultural Theory*, London 2000, p. 121, n. 14.

10   Herbert Marcuse, 'The Affirmative Character of Culture', in *Negations: Essays in Critical Theory*, London 1968, pp. 88–133.

11   'Sensibility' seems historically more appropriate as a translation of Marcuse's *Seele* than the literal 'soul' of the English edition.

12   Marcuse, *Negations*, pp. 132–3.

characteristically, was less inclined to anticipate a transformed existence or to coordinate his vision with any collective political prospectus. In a critical sequel drafted some years after Marcuse's study, he
traced a different path beyond culture, involving another kind of
practice. Negation, for him too, is the 'very truth' of culture. 'Just
because culture affirms the validity of the principle of harmony
within an antagonistic society . . . it cannot avoid confronting society with its own notion of harmony and thereby stumbling on
discord.' But the outcome of the confrontation is paralysis: culture
turns on itself, and the labour of the negative is confined to the
agitated stasis that is Kulturkritik. The critic 'is necessarily of the
same essence as that to which he fancies himself superior . . . His
vanity aids that of culture: even in the accusing gesture, the critic
clings to the notion of culture, isolated, unquestioned, dogmatic.'[13]
Yet, as the moment in which culture comes to perceive the discrepancy between its empirical generality and its 'principle', Kulturkritik
is not worthless. It brings 'untruth to consciousness of itself', and in
that lies its own 'truth'. The proper task of 'dialectical' thought that
'does not wish to succumb to "Economism"' is not to catalogue
and condemn Kulturkritik but to 'absorb' it. Dialectical criticism
differs from Kulturkritik in that it 'heightens' it, 'until the notion of
culture is itself negated, fulfilled and surmounted in one'.

Immanent Critique and Regression

Not many Marxist critiques of culture have been so free of super-
stition, or so confident that philistines are other people. And yet
dialectical reason can sometimes appear to practise its own kind
of magic—*Aufhebung* as verbal legerdemain. It is worth inquiring
just how much, in the Frankfurt critique and specifically in
Adorno's 'immanent criticism of culture', was cancelled, and how
much preserved.

The constitutive tension of immanent critique is manifest in its
self-designation. As immanent, it 'bores from within', unlike

---

13 Theodor W. Adorno, 'Cultural Criticism and Society', in *Prisms*, Cambridge,
MA, 1981, pp. 28, 27, 19.

'transcendent criticism', which renounces 'a spontaneous relation to the object' in the name of an 'external', supervenient truth. Yet as critique, it must exceed the categories implied in the object; empathy, so to say, is procedural, a strong tactic, not a means to final identification. At once inside and outside, immanent critique is not so much a position as an ethic of movement, a critical practice whose artistic analogue would be music of a kind.[14] Its tension is then 'dialectical'—or could be, but only in so far as the force of negation is sufficient to sustain the movement, if the conceptual 'outside' is more than a figment. It is not easy to conclude that Adorno believed this—or, in impersonal terms, that his concepts can quite admit the thought. 'Transcendental criticism'—his estranging philosophical term for the prevailing styles of Marxism—takes its stand on non-existent ground. Where 'ideology' has saturated the whole, as he maintains it has, there is no outside: the idea is 'an abstract utopia', a 'fiction', an Archimedean dream. Orthodoxy clings to its illusion at the cost of regression to pre-cultural 'nature' and scientism. But how, then, can Adorno's ethic of critical movement continue to mark its difference from the futile agitations of Kulturkritik, and at what cost to itself?

The master-concept in Adornian critical theory is exchange: the commodity form, with its barely limitable power of reification, is the nuclear reality of capitalism as a whole. The historic momentum of society is registered in another canonical concept, that of the productive forces and their development. But where so-called orthodoxy saw the material promise—or even the guarantee—of an emancipating socialism, Adorno saw only a system of frustrations. Again and again, his essays move towards the same final cadence. A retrospective discussion of Spengler invokes 'the powerless, . . . the negative embodiment within the negativity of this culture of everything which promises, however feebly, to break the dictatorship of culture and put an end to the horror of prehistory. In their protest lies the only hope that fate and power will

---

14   In contrast with Lukács, whose criticism is governed by the visual image of perspective: dialectics is 'the point of view of totality', from which historical representations—those of the novel above all—can be surveyed, placed and assessed.

not have the last word.' Of Thorstein Veblen he concludes: 'He represents poverty. This is his truth, because men are still constrained to be poor, and his untruth, because the absurdity of poverty has become manifest. Today, adjustment to what is possible no longer means adjustment; it means making the possible real.' Elsewhere, he spoke wistfully of a liberation 'near enough to touch'.[15] Such passages at once recall and displace the kind of closing ceremony that has been traditional in Marxist prose. 'Valedictory flourish' is the stock description, and it does not fit. These are visions of a promise that mocks hope. Creaturely enough for all his rigour, in such gestures Adorno delays the moment of parting, the last goodbye to the only bearable future.

In theoretical logic, it could only be so. The franchise of commodities and the chained promise of social productivity are the counterpart structural effects of capitalist property—a concept certainly present to Adorno yet, crucially, inactive in his reasoning. The 'dictatorship' sustaining 'pre-history' is that of a class, whose social other, not merely (or necessarily) 'poor' and not merely (or necessarily) 'powerless', is above all propertyless, the wage-labouring collective producer of social existence. This constitutive social antagonism appears only negatively in Adorno's work, in the forms of its putative neutralization. It was the division of mental and manual labour, rather, that furnished the terms of his engagement in the stand-off between committed and autonomous art, between all autonomous endeavour and the culture industry.[16] In politics proper, an unqualifiable leftism underwrote a critical ethic of remoteness. As he wrote very late in his life, defending his practice against the reproaches of the student movement, 'at the present moment, no higher form of society is concretely visible: for that reason anything that seems in easy reach is regressive'. And regression, 'objectively viewed', is renunciation.[17] His judgement

15   Adorno, *Prisms*, pp. 72, 94.

16   See Theodor W. Adorno, *Dialectic of Enlightenment* (with Max Horkheimer), London 1972, and 'Commitment', in *Notes to Literature*, vol. 2, New York 1992, pp. 76–94.

17   Theodor W. Adorno, 'Resignation', in *The Culture Industry*, ed. J. M. Bernstein, London 1991, p. 174.

on Carl Schmitt suggested an alienation still more fundamental than this self-cancelling maximalism. Again appealing to the notion of regression, he dismissed 'the *a priori* reduction to the friend–enemy relationship' and concluded: 'Freedom would be not to choose between black and white but to abjure such choices.'[18]

If there is an Adornian politics, its utopian disposition is precisely *un*political, in Mann's approving sense. And that is not the only sign of affinity with Kulturkritik. Marxist though he was, Adorno's vision of modernity as a closed system of productivity and exchange might have given the anti-Marxist Leavis cause for second thoughts. In a prose that is for the greater part unbendingly objective, in the literary sense, the personae that sometimes flicker are worth noting. Adorno rejects the practice of class-ascriptive tagging in Marxist criticism, that 'topological thinking, which knows the place of every phenomenon and the essence of none'. But there is more than one way of outing the socially unspeakable, as his own critical language suggests. 'Most socialist contributions to cultural criticism . . . lack the experience of that with which they deal'; 'they develop an affinity to barbarism'; their theoretical tenets 'take on a backwoods ring'.[19] Not quite 'petty bourgeois', then, but perhaps not even that. The voice that delivers these judgements comes from elsewhere. 'To anyone in the habit of thinking with his ears', Adorno begins, 'the words "cultural criticism" (*Kulturkritik*) must have an offensive ring'—and 'not merely because, like "automobile", they are pieced together from Latin and Greek'.[20] Here, pitch-perfect, is an epitome of the cultural principle: music *contra* Fordism and the half-educated. That the trope of discrimination is reminiscent of Henry James, and the philology already an old school-room dogma, is essential to the ambiguous feeling of the passage. It is proof that Adorno's immanent critique, unsure of the 'outside' possibility that would fuel its dialectical movement, was not spared the general curse of regression—in his case, to the natural aristocratism of Kulturkritik.

---

18   Theodor W. Adorno, *Minima Moralia*, London 1974, p. 132.
19   Adorno, *Prisms*, pp. 33, 32.
20   Ibid., p. 19. The English edition incorporates the German term.

Ambiguities of Utopia

Marcuse, in contrast, persisted in his search for keys that might unlock 'the enchained possibilities' of the present. His estimate of historical probabilities was scarcely more optimistic than Adorno's. In the early 1930s, he would say no more than that 'the fate of the labour movement is clouded with uncertainty'.[21] By the middle sixties, the landscape was sunlit but barren:

> these possibilities are gradually being realized through means and institutions which cancel their liberating potential, and this process affects not only the means but also the ends. The instruments of productivity and progress, organized into a totalitarian system, determine not only the actual but also the possible utilizations. At its most advanced stage, domination functions as administration, and in the overdeveloped areas of mass consumption, the administered life becomes the good life of the whole, in the defence of which the opposites are united.[22]

Yet Marcuse's political conclusion was defiant, and implicitly activist: a genuinely liberating socialism would have to imagine a transformation far more comprehensive than that envisaged in the classical programmes. 'Freedom is only possible as the realization of what today is called utopia.'[23]

Advanced capitalism, as Marcuse theorizes it in *One-Dimensional Man*, is more truly 'totalitarian' than fascism ever was. The central concept of the analysis is no longer quite Marx's 'productive forces'—important though this theoretical reference is, in his writing as in Adorno's. It is 'the technological apparatus', which subsumes property and productivity, forms of power as well as concentrations of wealth, under a single category, the

21   Marcuse, 'The Struggle against Liberalism in the Totalitarian View of the State', 1934, in *Negations*, p. 42.
22   Herbert Marcuse, *One-Dimensional Man*, London 1964, p. 199.
23   Marcuse, *Negations*, p. xx.

self-sustaining increase in mastery over nature and society, or domination. (Here again, comparison with Leavis is apt.) In a universe so cohesive, so tightly sealed, it seems impossible that a sufficient counterforce might gather, let alone prevail as 'the new Subject' of history. Even culture has lost its negative role, operating now as an agency of 'repressive desublimation'. Yet there, precisely, is the point from which Marcuse launches his dialectics of liberation. The third and last part of *One-Dimensional Man*, where a less thought-prone spirit might have positioned an exposition of the historical function of the proletariat, opens with a crucial account of 'the historical commitment of philosophy'. In a remarkable speculative sequence, Marcuse explores a process in which, by virtue of technical development, ideas once set aside as metaphysical become scientific, and science itself, with technical reason no longer alienated from art, turns finalistic, thus constituting a new theory and practice of politics. All this process lacks is an enabling social subject.

In 1937, Marcuse had seen bourgeois 'culture' as an ambiguous sign of alienation, whose vanishing point would coincide with the actuality of freedom. Now it appeared that a certain dialectic of culture and the technological apparatus would be essential to the work of transformation. Far from overcoming the ancient opposition between the liberal and useful arts—the point of departure for the critique of affirmative culture—socialism would canonize it, or so Marcuse seems to say, in the closing pages of *One-Dimensional Man*:

> Self-determination in the production and distribution of vital goods and services would be wasteful. The job is a technical one, and as a truly technical job, it makes for the reduction of physical and mental toil. In this realm, centralized control is rational if it establishes the preconditions for meaningful self-determination. The latter can become effective in its own realm—in the decisions which involve the production and distribution of the economic surplus, and in the individual existence.[24]

---

24 Marcuse, *One-Dimensional Man*, p. 197.

If utopian theory is normally ambiguous, then here it develops by its bad side. In this culminating vision, the relation between necessary and surplus production appears as a valorized institutional differentiation in economic, cultural and political life. There is regression here. This programmatic division is no more sustainable than the orthodox prospectus of a transition from 'the government of persons' to the 'administration of things and the direction of the process of production'[25]—to which, in substance, it returns. Things, as social values, are never dissociable from persons, except in the fictions of consensus by which bureaucracies routinely validate the prerogatives of their experts; the phrase 'vital goods and services' is itself redolent of official communiqués, and the hard measures to be taken, as they always are, in the best interests of all. The 'toil' so spared us is the necessary work of a socialist democracy.

That Marcuse should have reasoned as he did is nevertheless consistent with his spontaneous cultural inclination, in which, again, utopia entailed regression. The prevalence of 'culture' as good tender is an index of alienated potentiality, he had maintained. However, he now appeared to say, freedom from necessity must include exemption from the care and effort of thinking about it. The putative sphere of necessity, by contrastive implication, is meaningless. The reality is otherwise. Social 'necessity' is excessively meaningful, inherently ambiguous and often contentiously so. Marcuse acknowledged as much in his (questionable) concept of 'artificial needs'. The idea that the technical and moral arts of necessity are a vexation beneath the dignity of a self-determining commonwealth is a delusion, but one that runs back, as he tells us, to Aristotle. His image of liberation is a palimpsest of the ages: revolutionary seizure and remaking of the

---

25 Friedrich Engels, *Anti-Dühring*, cit. V. I. Lenin, *The State and Revolution*, Peking 1965, p. 19. Compare Marx's discriminations, in *Capital*, vol. 3, between the realms of 'necessity' and 'freedom' and the intermediate state of freedom-in-necessity (London 1981, p. 959)—a passage which, although it may well have inspired Marcuse's thinking, does not warrant the idea of an institutionalized differentiation in social practice. Of course, the context of Marx's discussion was not programmatic.

technological apparatus, the realization of affirmative culture, aristocratic privilege for all.

III. Metaculture and Politics

Marxism did not emerge unchanged from this 'immanent' engagement with culture, which, as Kulturkritik, re-inflected the concepts that entered its gravitational field, so shaping a distinctive theoretical orbit. The Frankfurt critique of culture, for all its piercing insight, participates in metacultural discourse. This is not a statement of the obvious, in my view, nor is it easily specified without distortion. But on Stefan Collini's reading, it would be a necessary implication of a truth that I do not acknowledge: '*Discourse about metacultural discourse*', he writes, in criticism of my basic thesis, '*is still a form of metacultural discourse*.'[26] Now there speaks metacultural discourse. That emphatic contention crowns a passage of argument in which Collini re-accents the core vocabulary of the book, retrieving *culture* and *politics*—and *metaculture* too—in senses more congenial to himself, and, it must be said, the broad tradition of Kulturkritik.

Of course, our disagreement is about concepts, not a word. 'Metaculture' is not my coinage, and the sense I give it does not drive out others. A rarefied word, by virtue of its etymology (which would make Adorno wince), in fact it is current in a half-dozen or more senses today, ranging as high and as low as its mother-term. In evolutionary psychology and anthropology, metaculture signifies 'the bedrock of universals' or 'the operating system' on which any actual culture depends; it circulates in a similar sense in discussion of Hermann Hesse's cult novel *The Glass Bead Game*; it is the title of a series of leisure guides, and has legal standing as the proprietary name of a US postcard business, Metaculture™. In the perspective of linguistic usage, *meta* might as well mean 'parody'. Blessedly unaware of all this, I recoined 'metaculture' as the summarizing term of a critical thesis, which is what matters

---

26 'Culture Talk', above, p. 41, italics in original.

here. If Collini's counterclaim holds good, if the critique of meta-cultural discourse is, so to say, necessarily and wholly immanent, then the thesis fails.

The immediate appeal of Collini's objection lies in its phrasing, which highlights the *reflexivity* of the critical operation. Indeed, this is not sufficient to ground a distinction between metaculture and other forms of critical discourse on culture. And even if, as he agrees, the criterion of *generality* remains central, there still seems little reason for a strong distinction between metacultural discourse and other, comparably synoptic work in, say, sociology or anthropology. On the first count, 'metaculture' is theoretically redundant, a word in search of a concept; on the second count, its purchase is merely descriptive. However, metaculture has a third property, the crucial one, in so far as it welds and charges the other two: it asserts a *cultural principle*. Metacultural discourse is strongly reflexive in that its subject and object are one and the same culture, now split between norm and actuality. Its generality is tendentious, signifying a claim to authority over the social whole. In that subject and that generality, culture-as-principle anticipates the end of politics.

Here Collini struggles to find his ground. The critical appeal to 'culture' need not presuppose a 'given or transcendent locus of value', he maintains. But the formulations in which he sets out his position are circular. 'Disciplined reflection partly grounded in an extensive intellectual and aesthetic inheritance can furnish a place to stand' in 'critical engagement' with politics.[27] It cannot. In the Arnoldian problematic that governs Collini's reasoning at this point, the first phrase is no more than an elaboration of the second. No other kind of engagement could be critical in the required sense, and the question of a place—a location in the contested order of social value—remains unanswered. Culture 'still names an essential ethical move', he insists, 'an allusion to the bearing which that kind of disinterested or autotelic exploration of human possibility, characteristically (but not exclusively) pursued in artis-tic and intellectual activity, can have upon those processes that are

---

27   Ibid., above, p. 40.

governed by the need to bring about proximate instrumental ends'.[28] This assertion simply assumes what it needs to establish. The word 'characteristically' is an ideological wand. Marcuse might have seized on it to illustrate the transmutation of the historical generality of art and ideas into a transcendent value whose content is its negation of the realm of interests, or 'affirmative culture'. Contrary to Collini's unmistakable intentions in the matter, the place of critical engagement turns out to be another world.

Ideas of Politics

The reinvention of Arnold's cultural principle finds its necessary complement in a renewed depreciation of politics: the phrase 'proximate instrumental ends' is characteristic. 'Politics', in the language of Collini's critique, is a negative value, normally qualified as 'everyday', 'instrumental', 'present-driven', or pejoratively associated with 'narrow pragmatism' and 'partial or specialized perspectives'.[29] It is the lesser moral reality against which culture-as-subject exercises its power of general reflection. The concept of metacultural discourse presupposes a different understanding of politics.

If the banal evidence of parliamentary affairs is desolating, the negative generalizations routinely derived from it are only a little less so. A properly critical concept of politics should trace the horizon of possibility—what is conceivable as politics—as one condition of its theoretical sufficiency. Metacultural claims then appear differently. Politics is the struggle to determine the totality of social relations in a given space (which may or may not coincide with a state territory). It presupposes at least an intuition of the whole. In this sense, the formal characteristics that Collini reserves for a certain ethic of 'culture' are, in truth, the 'everyday', because constitutive, reality of politics, which is general, qualitative labour on social relations. The basic temporalities of politics are

---

28   Ibid., examples to be found on pp. 40, 36, 39.
29   Ibid., pp. 48–51, *passim*.

maintenance and transformation. (Restoration is not a true third, being in effect a phantasmatic rendering of one or the other of those two.) The narrowness and pragmatism that Collini associates with politics as such will inevitably be more pronounced in conditions where the dominant temporality is maintenance, and still more where that is consensual—where the fundamental qualities of the social order have been naturalized. However, the exceptional case of transformation illuminates the general reality. Lenin assumed just this, in arguing that a revolutionary party would only be truly revolutionary if it was truly political, if it measured itself against the state, in organizational reach but also in the form of its vision, learning to see social relations as the state, in principle, 'sees' them, in the round. At the heart of *What Is to Be Done?*, animating its better-known organizational arguments, is an idea of politics as general labour, as a theory and practice of synopsis.

This is not to say that politics is distinctive, or distinctive only, for its exercise of the synoptic faculty—which, on the contrary, can be seen at work in every register of a cultural formation, and, conspicuously, in the leading genres of culture-as-principle. Political synopsis differentiates itself within that generality by virtue of its constitutive relation to practice, to the maintenance or transformation of actual social relations.

Whatever its medium or site, political discourse as such is predominantly deliberative in orientation and, explicitly or not, injunctive in its address. That is what I intended in saying that politics is 'modally specialized'. I now regret that innocent phrase. Mentally stressing the first word, I overlooked the colloquial drift of the second—from specificity to professionalism—with unfortunate results. Collini is perhaps only teasing when he offers 'specialism' as an equivalent for his own phrase, 'narrow pragmatism'. Bruce Robbins, though standing in a different relation to pragmatism, makes the same reading, and in earnest. Finding in *Metaculture* an attempt to 'correct' the 'anti-democratic tendency in the social criticism of the past century', he warns that the 'desire to reinstate politics in the specialized sense makes this even more difficult. For specialization in the domain of politics will value certain people and skills above others, just as specialization in the domain of culture does . . . In short, there is no escape from culture to politics.'[30]

Indeed there is not. Once culture is understood, as it is in *Metaculture*, as the moment of sense-making in all social relations, the very idea of escape becomes self-contradictory. The real issue is the discursive action of the cultural *principle*—which in Robbins's case, as in that of cultural studies generally, is a popular value—in the plane of contested social authority, and specifically in that of politics as a specific form of practice. That dimension of the concept of metaculture simply disappears, in his passing summary of it, returning at length in the unappealing figure of the old-style politico, a left-culturalist bogey to match Collini's narrow pragmatist. Politics is ordinary, Robbins might well say, echoing the high tradition of cultural studies, and so it is, but not in the same way as culture itself. Culture is everywhere; politics can be anywhere, and that is not the same thing. Any social antagonism can become political, Schmitt maintained, in the sense of intensifying to the point where it assumes the defining form of politics: a public and collective friend–enemy relationship pursued in consciousness of the 'possibility of the extreme case', the 'fight to the death'.[31] If Schmitt's philosophical embrace of mortal combat is ideological, a decadent foreclosure of the possibility of a pacified social existence, his rigorous formalism yields an insight from which there is something to learn. It is not the formalism of *Metaculture*, where the context of thought was given by Lenin and Gramsci, but the implications run parallel. If the specific difference of politics is *formal*, not a matter of social substance, still less of rarefied professional arts, then the culture–politics relation is one internal to each of the related terms. Cultural complexes inhabit politics as the field and uncertain horizon of what is socially imaginable; and the practices of identity and representation, the patternings of affinity and aversion, that make up these

---

30   Bruce Robbins, 'No Escape', *London Review of Books*, 1 November 2001, p. 35.

31   Carl Schmitt, *The Concept of the Political*, Chicago and London 1996, p. 35.

complexes are always, in principle, textured by the possibility of politics, as threat or demand or opportunity.

Politics can thus be anywhere, yet not, like culture, everywhere. For if politics is indeed formally *specific*, then what is internalized is precisely a relation, which presupposes non-identity. Political practice is *trans*-cultural in its re-working of value as demand, sometimes promoting given identities and preferences, sometimes rearticulating or disturbing or backgrounding them, according to judgements based on a socially determinate programme and strategy. The commonalities and antagonisms it elaborates do not simply express or prefigure desirable ways of life. They define agencies and stakes in a struggle for collective advance on the given social terrain. Deliberately culturalized politics is only apparently different in this. So-called lifestyle politics acquires political efficacy only in so far as it assumes means and modes of contention that the lifestyle does not itself include and may not even value. The literary spectacles of the Popular Front in the 1930s and the 'deconstructive' street ballet of the *tute bianche*, for all their contrasts of sensibility and circumstances, illustrate the same apparent paradox: 'culture', as it enters directly into the space of political practice, negates its ideal self-image, becoming a tactic. If Comintern instrumentalism can be cited in part-explanation of the earlier case, no equivalent suspect can be found in the later one, which continues an antithetical, expressivist tradition of militancy. The cultural *mise en abyme* is implicit in the logic of politics as an autonomous form of social practice.

'Discrepancy' is the term I have used to summarize the limits and possibilities of the relationship, and to qualify the meanings of 'cultural politics'. Seen in this light, cultural politics is not a position, or even a demarcated set of practices; it is an inescapable field of forces whose dynamism is constantly renewed by the non-identity of its constituent terms; it is the discrepancy and its effects. Structured by discrepancy, cultural politics is a space of frustration but also, and in the same measure, of creativity. The processes by which a mythic battle of the sexes was turned into the women's liberation movement, and then a broader, more diverse feminism, are a classic demonstration of this. The unwriting of the working class, as subject and interest, in the discourse of social-liberal modernity, is another impressive demonstration, and a reminder that creativity is not only a good thing. Such precedents are there for socialists to ponder, as they face their own unknowns, chief among them the shapes of an adequate—imaginative and capable—contemporary politics.

4

STEFAN COLLINI

Defending Cultural Criticism

In the activity described by the rather tired phrase 'an intellectual exchange', it is too often the case that all the protagonists manage to give each other is a piece of their minds. They exchange shots but don't, in any genuine sense, 'exchange' ideas, the participants generally resembling incorrigible Bourbons. Recognizing this risk, I nonetheless want to try to respond to Francis Mulhern's reply to my reading of his book *Culture/Metaculture*, encouraged by the belief that our earlier contributions have already gone some way towards escaping this dispiriting pattern. Certainly, Mulhern's reply is acute, constructive and, to pinch one of his own kind phrases, 'generous beyond ordinary expectation'. Moreover, in clarifying and extending his position, he throws down a funda-mental challenge to anyone who, like me, thinks they believe there is a legitimate role for something called 'cultural criticism', as opposed to Mulhern's 'cultural politics'; so, trying to go a little further in identifying where we agree and where we differ may at least provide some grist to others' mills.

The central argument of Mulhern's book, in his own careful summary, is as follows:

Metaculture names a modern discursive formation in which 'culture', however understood, speaks of its own generality and historical conditions of existence. Its inherent strategic impulse—failing which it would be no more than descriptive anthropology—is to mobilize 'culture' as a principle against the prevailing generality of 'politics' in the disputed plane of social authority. What speaks in metacultural discourse is the cultural principle itself, as it strives to dissolve the political as locus of general arbitration in social relations. Kulturkritik and Cultural Studies, typically contrasting in social attachment yet sharing this discursive template, have been strong versions of this metacultural will to authority. For the left, such logic is either inimical or self-defeating.[1]

In my earlier essay, while emphasizing the merits of the book as a whole, I raised both a historical and a theoretical objection to these claims. In 'Beyond Metaculture' Mulhern now responds strongly to these objections, and then elaborates and extends his original argument; but he does so in ways that, for me at least, make it seem less rather than more persuasive. I shall try to address the issues, broadly in the order in which Mulhern raises them, but I shall then go on to touch on what seem to me the even larger underlying questions, ultimately questions about the role, and the limits, of intellectual work in relation to public debate.

In what follows, I do not take myself to be saying anything particularly novel or to be staking out a distinctively personal position. My concern, rather, is that the tightly interlaced grid of concepts through which Mulhern makes his criticisms of what he calls 'metacultural discourse' involves a baby-with-the-bathwater outcome: in other words, it appears to eliminate the possibility, or at least deny the legitimacy, of what has conventionally been called 'cultural criticism'. I am well aware that this term is now used in many senses, especially within American academia,[2] but I believe the traditional sense is also still usable and useful—the sense associated, in Britain, with aspects of the work of figures such as Matthew Arnold, T. S. Eliot, George Orwell, Richard Hoggart, and so on. Contemporary versions of cultural criticism, in this sense, still seem to me to have a valuable part to play in public

---

1 'Beyond Metaculture', above, pp. 45–6.

2 For American usage see, for example, Gerald Graff and Bruce Robbins, 'Cultural Criticism', in Stephen Greenblatt and Giles Gunn, eds, *Redrawing the Boundaries: The Transformation of English and American Literary Studies*, New York 1992.

debate, and the effect of Mulhern's argument—especially in its restated form—appears to be to deny any standing to this activity.

Necessarily, this exchange must deploy a number of large and contested abstract categories, and there is always a danger that too much may appear to turn on stipulative definition. When one of us proposes a category of 'cultural politics', to which the other responds by insisting on the desirability of continuing to speak of 'cultural criticism', it may seem a case of the narcissism of small differences. But within the broad area of our common concerns there is, I believe, a genuine and relatively fundamental disagreement at stake, and such disagreement is bound to be expressed partly through matters of intellectual allegiance and preferred vocabulary.

The term 'culture' itself is the most worrying but also the most intractable of these categories, and I have perhaps even more worries than Mulhern about whether it is practicable to treat the various senses as belonging to a single semantic field. In what follows, I shall try to restrict my own invocations of 'culture' to what Raymond Williams, in the book both Mulhern and I would recognize as having set the terms for so much modern discussion (for better or, as I would hold about some aspects of it, for worse), called 'the primary' meaning, namely, 'artistic and intellectual activities'.[3] I am obviously not denying that there are all sorts of purposes for which it is entirely legitimate to take 'culture' in one of its other senses, as Mulhern does in much of his discussion and as I myself do on other occasions. But where the enterprise of 'cultural criticism' and its relation to 'politics' (another of these deceptively familiar abstractions) are in question, there is at least a certain utility to beginning with this narrower sense of 'culture'. I shall hereafter do so without using the question marks that signal my recognition that this is only one of the term's several meanings.

---

3   Raymond Williams, *Culture and Society 1780–1950*, London 1958, p. xvii.

I. The Category of Kulturkritik

The term 'Kulturkritik' is used by Mulhern in a specific and some-what idiosyncratic sense. I suggested, in slightly minatory tones, that it is important to recognize that the term, when so used, 'designates a position or tradition that has been constructed by Mulhern himself'. He returns by contending that all such general concepts are 'constructions': the real issue, he argues, concerns its nature and 'its claim to rational plausibility'.[4]

General concepts may indeed be 'constructions' in some sense, but where they are being used to characterize a slice of the past, 'rational plausibility' may not be enough. First of all, there is a special reason for drawing attention to the constructed nature of Mulhern's category, in that the term with which he labels it has *already* had a long and well-established history in an overlapping, but not identical, sense that refers to a distinctively Germanic tradition of social thinking. He is attempting to appropriate the term and to redefine its meaning and its historical range. This courts confusion: he *may* persuade some others to use the term in his special, theoretically defined, sense, though the room for slip-page seems invitingly wide. Of course, the label *'Kulturkritik'*, as applied to certain contemporary, non-German, examples of cultural commentary, does already make occasional appearances in English-language writing, and it would seem to me an unneces-sarily purist restriction on our vocabulary to object to this allusive usage. But allusion is not concept-formation. When the term is used in this relatively relaxed way (as applied to, say, the work of Allan Bloom or George Steiner), it functions rather as a citation, often ironic. In such cases, part of the appeal of the usage is precisely the self-conscious borrowing of a term acknowledged to have a culturally and historically located referent. Mulhern, by contrast, wants both to naturalize the term and to give it a more determinate conceptual structure.

But, beyond this, all kinds of categories may possess 'rational plausibility' yet be historically distorting. Mulhern specifies his

---

4 'Beyond Metaculture', above, p. 47.

category 'morphologically': it is constituted by a recurring structural relation among concepts such as culture, politics, authority. But for it to function effectively as a way of organizing our *historical* understanding and to pick out a 'tradition', as he more than once refers to it, we would need to know much more about the place of this set of conceptual relations in the work of the different figures who are said to make up 'the tradition of Kulturkritik'. Does it play some central or energizing part in their work, or is it peripheral—or barely discernible? Is it consistent with the general thrust of the writings in which it is discerned, or at odds with it? Are the concepts among which the allegedly recurrent relation obtains actually constant across significant chronological and cultural variations? Is the alleged common pattern recognized as such by the supposed members of this tradition—and if not, why not? Does its use illuminate more than it distorts? And so on. Mulhern's category of Kulturkritik is a polemical weapon, one that is central to the scheme of his book. But to emphasize that it is indeed his own construction, and one formulated at quite a high level of abstraction, is neither an expression of obtuse nominalism nor a resistance to conceptual innovation. It is to register that such constructions have to pass demanding tests before they can expect to be naturalized in the historian's vocabulary, and 'rational plausibility' is only one of those tests.

Following the emphasis of *Culture/Metaculture*, which starts its historical survey in 1918, I initially took Mulhern's focus to be on the European inter-war cultural pessimists, and I queried his building their particular form of cultural alarmism and social conservatism into the category itself.[5] His subsequent clarification of the scope of the category of Kulturkritik, and his insistence that it has no particular political or social affiliations, conservative or otherwise, is helpful in one way, but somewhat unnerving in another. In the Introduction to his book, Mulhern

---

5 I am slightly comforted by the fact that so sympathetic a critic as Bruce Robbins also construed the book's historical argument as an attempt to 'correct' the 'antidemocratic tendency in the social criticism of the past century': Robbins, 'No Escape', p. 35.

had already mentioned in passing that Kulturkritik, as he uses it, is to be traced back to the late eighteenth century, and that its English 'tradition' is that discussed in Williams's *Culture and Society*. But he has now extended it in other directions, most notably by his elaboration of a form of the tradition absent from the original book, namely 'the disconcerting possibility [*Culture/ Metaculture*] appeared to exclude in advance, that of a Marxist Kulturkritik'.[6]

I shall return in a moment to the question of why Mulhern might regard this as a 'disconcerting' possibility, but what I believe would disconcert most intellectual historians is the sheer range of types of writing this category is now being asked to cover. After all, Williams's own (very questionable) elaboration of 'the culture-and-society tradition' ranged from Burke and Cobbett, through Mill and Newman, to Eliot and Orwell. Mulhern's category now extends this, not only to embrace figures running from Herder to Mann, but, in other directions, to include the likes of Benda and Ortega; and, now, Adorno and Marcuse. To ask for detailed discussion of all these figures and their cultural milieux would, I agree, be to ask for 'another kind of work' than that which Mulhern has undertaken; but it still seems to me a legitimate reservation to say that the extent to which these very diverse figures 'acted within a shared discursive order and subserved its governing logic'—and, above all, what the interpretive status of this 'governing logic' is, when its exemplars are so diverse—remains open to question.[7] Of course we need organizing concepts to be able to write history at all; but the potential weakness of this notion of a 'discursive formation' is that it grants the later interpreter an authority to discern examples of its 'logic' in a way that overrides *all* discriminations made in the vocabulary of the periods in question. It can then become difficult to see what kinds of textual evidence could be acknowledged as challenging the appropriateness of the initial category.

There also remains some unclarity, it seems to me, about both

6 Mulhern, *Culture/Metaculture*, p. xvi; 'Beyond Metaculture', above, p. 52.
7 'Beyond Metaculture', above, p. 47.

the relation of Kulturkritik to its parent category of 'metacultural discourse' and the defining marks of Kulturkritik itself. To
begin with, there is the question of whether Kulturkritik and
Cultural Studies are merely two among several illustrations of
the larger category—and, if so, what other examples there might
be—or whether, taken together, they exhaustively constitute it.
(In 'Beyond Metaculture' Mulhern, understandably, focuses on
his claims about Kulturkritik rather than upon his provocative
identification of a comparable conceptual structure at work in
Cultural Studies. I shall follow this emphasis here, although in a
larger discussion one might need to reconsider this linkage in the
light of what Mulhern acknowledges as the 'authoritarian bearing' of Kulturkritik.) Then there is the question of whether
metacultural discourse/Kulturkritik is defined purely structurally, or whether it has any determinate content. In summarizing
the argument of his book Mulhern again emphasizes the priority
of form, in terms of

> the recurrence of certain relations among concepts (culture,
> politics, authority), a certain array of topoi (modernity as disin-
> tegration, for example), a certain ethos of address (the prophetic
> intellectual and kindred personae).[8]

But it is not obvious that these *are* all 'formal' characteristics.
The topos of 'modernity as disintegration', for example, specifies a particular type of content, one which, when joined to his
suggestion that Kulturkritik is marked by its taste for 'climacterics' and the ensuing 'general alert', still seems to justify my
suggestion, repudiated by Mulhern, that the tradition as he
describes it is represented as 'culturally alarmist'. (It is also,
incidentally, an ingredient that seems more plausibly characteristic of Kulturkritik alone than of 'metacultural discourse'
more generally.) Indeed, at several points Mulhern seems to
give Kulturkritik a set of historically located characteristics
that are all more than formal. For example, he suggests that,

---

8   Ibid., above, p. 47.

for the proponents of Kulturkritik, the culminating feature of modernity was 'the rise of the masses', and elsewhere he claims that 'intuitions of loss define the temporal imagination of Kulturkritik'. This then raises questions about the minimal criteria for membership of the tradition. He later wishes that, in a more extended account, one might 'probe the significance of a thinker such as Croce, whose thought has some formal affinity with Kulturkritik, but perhaps no more substantial association'. This again seems to indicate that the category is to be specified in more than purely formal terms. And, finally, this surely explains why it is the 'classic critics of "mass" modernity' that provide the 'canonical texts' of this tradition.[9] Mulhern's category has been extended outwards from a core that did, indeed, have a historical existence, not just a 'rational plausibility', but some of the features specific to this historical instance seem to have been retained within the larger redefinition.

A Metacultural Marxism?

Obviously, the most notable extension of the category suggested in Mulhern's recent article is that of a Marxist Kulturkritik. I am not confident that I altogether follow his discussion here, but he seems to be suggesting that Adorno and Marcuse shared a common failing, one that is homologous with that identified in his earlier examples of Kulturkritik. The fundamental limitation of Adorno's work, he argues, was an inability to find anything in present society upon which to ground his dialectical criticism, and hence no basis for a progressive view of the future. As a result, his critique of contemporary society becomes regressive, re-enacting the 'natural aristocratism of Kulturkritik'. Marcuse's disdain of the 'realm of necessity', his locating of the realization of human potential above or outside any mechanisms actually present in the dynamics of social life, seems to condemn him to a similar cul-de-sac. The ultimate unrealism of

9   See Mulhern, *Culture/Metaculture*, pp. 4, 161, xx, and above, p. 40.

his hope for the future is characterized as 'aristocratic privilege for all'.[10]

The recurrence of 'aristocratic' in these charges illuminates something further about Mulhern's category of Kulturkritik. Although he insists that Kulturkritik is 'politically changeable'—able to appear in 'conservative, liberal, or socialist' varieties, and not 'uniformly "conservative" or "reactionary"'—his extension of the category here does suggest it always exhibits a 'regressive' quality that helps to foster attitudes most readers would recognize as broadly conservative in character. The relation between the critic and the forms of life being criticized, between the writer and the public, is at the heart of this; and it is, as we shall see, a relation that Mulhern regards as inherently 'elitist'. So, although he insists that the 'logic' of Kulturkritik may, as a matter of (so to say) contingent historical fact, have been accompanied by more or less any political allegiance in any given writer, a particular—and, to Mulhern, particularly offensive—political bearing does appear to be built into the category itself.

This is borne out, it seems to me, by Mulhern's acknowledgement that the possibility of a Marxist Kulturkritik is to be regarded as 'disconcerting'. Why, after all, should it be so, if the category has no necessary political affiliation? It is surely because, in Mulhern's redefinition, there is a more fundamental tension between its alleged properties and those of Marxism than there is with any other position. Adorno and Marcuse, it seems, are being indicted for failing to relate their analyses to an actual politics which was attempting to organize those elements within the 'realm of necessity' that pointed towards a transformation of its present exploitative character. The identification of those elements and that character constitutes the core of Marxist theory. Any criticism of contemporary society from the standpoint of culture that is not grounded in a progressive analysis of class conflict is, it seems, inherently 'regressive'. The engagement with the organized expression of that conflict appears to be what 'politics' means here. What seems to be disconcerting about the cases of Adorno

---

10 'Beyond Metaculture', above, pp. 56, 60.

and Marcuse is that although they were working within an intellectual framework premised upon the possibility of transforming
existing social relations by means of such a politics, other elements
in their thought, especially a certain cultural hauteur, prevent
them from giving any coherent expression to that possibility.

All this suggests to me that the adoption of Mulhern's special,
extended sense of Kulturkritik as an organizing historical category would bring with it more drawbacks than benefits.
Successfully to embrace such a diverse range of figures, historical
categories other than those current at the time—including categories that adopt a label from the period but redefine its scope—need
to be fairly hospitable and easy-going, otherwise the redescription
involved will appear strained and unpersuasive. Kulturkritik, as
Mulhern uses it, is a category with a strong thesis built into its
very constitution; namely, that the defining move of those allegedly writing within this tradition is the attempt to 'displace' or
'sublimate' politics, indeed to 'dissolve political reason itself'. To
bring home the problems that use of this category would entail,
we need to move from my historical reservation to my theoretical
objection.

II. Dissolution of Politics

In 'Culture Talk', I challenged the description Mulhern gives of
his own argument in *Culture/Metaculture*. I suggested that his
discussion itself has to be seen as a further instalment of 'metacultural discourse'—not just because it is a form of intellectual
labour, but also because it is itself a reflective analysis of the place
of culture in public debate. In other words, I argued, it is not a
supersession of 'culture talk' by politics but rather a 'modern
meditation upon ... "the function of criticism"'. *'Discourse
about metacultural discourse'*, I insisted, in thumping italics, *'is
still a form of metacultural discourse.'*[11] I continue to think there
is a truth underlying this general characterization, but I would

---

11 'Culture Talk', above, p. 41.

now have to acknowledge that Mulhern is justified in saying of this section of my discussion that 'Collini re-accents the core vocabulary of the book, retrieving *culture* and *politics*—and *metaculture* too—in senses more congenial to himself'.[12] In particular, I think I underestimated the extent to which Mulhern's category of 'metaculture' does not just lend itself to, but is actually constituted by, a very strong thesis about the way in which the forms of cultural criticism he is analysing *entail* 'the dissolution of political reason itself' (whatever our other differences, Mulhern and I seem willing to agree that any blame for such misunderstandings, if blame there be, should be shared between us). As a result, my earlier italicized sentence now looks insensitive to the distinctive, and distinctively critical, character of the category; though this acknowledgement does not altogether settle the question of how far Mulhern's account is a further instalment of, rather than complete break with, the discourse he criticizes.

However, the further effect of this clarification is to make me feel that I was initially too indulgent towards Mulhern's use of the category. Roughly speaking (I shall try to make it a little less rough as I go on), the more tightly the conceptual circle is drawn, the less room there seems to be inside it for the forms of cultural criticism I would want to defend. For, in addition to the properties of generality and reflexivity that 'metaculture' shares with what Mulhern calls 'other forms of critical discourse on culture', he now emphasizes even more strongly that it is defined by a third quality: metaculture 'asserts a *cultural principle*', and 'culture-as-principle anticipates the end of politics'.[13] It now seems even more important than it did in my earlier reading of his book to bring out just how central to Mulhern's whole position this claim is—and to make clearer just where I disagree with it.

The repeated theme of Mulhern's writing—from the concluding chapter of *The Moment of 'Scrutiny'*, published in 1979, through some of the essays collected in *The Present Lasts a Long Time*, to *Culture/Metaculture* and his most recent *NLR* essay,

---

12 'Beyond Metaculture', above, p. 60.
13 Ibid., above, p. 61.

restating its argument—has been to reproach one or other historical example of cultural criticism for its failure to acknowledge or
express a 'real' politics, and hence, given his governing conceptual
economy, for its attempt to 'displace' politics as such. This failure
is represented as constitutive of what he calls 'the perceptual
scheme of liberal cultural criticism', in opposition to which he
constantly seeks to redeem or reinstate the dignity of 'politics'.[14]
This was the central, animating argument in his treatment of
Leavis and his circle in *The Moment of 'Scrutiny'*. There Mulhern
insisted that the reason why socialists should not regard *Scrutiny*
as a natural ally, despite certain superficial points of contact,

> is essentially that the basic and constant discursive organization
> of the journal, the matrix of its literary and cultural criticism
> and of its educational policies, of its radical and conservative
> manifestations alike, was one defined by a dialectic of 'culture'
> and 'civilization' whose *main* and *logically necessary effect* was
> a *depreciation*, a *repression*, and, at the limit, a *categorial disso-
> lution of politics as such*. Nothing could be more disorienting
> for socialist cultural theory than the ingestion of a discourse
> whose main effect is to undo the intelligibility of its ultimate
> concern: political mobilization against the existing structures
> of society and state.[15]

It is noticeable how the claim is already cast in apodictic terms: the
'constant' discursive organization of the journal was 'defined' by
a dialectic whose 'logically necessary' effect entailed 'a categorial
dissolution of politics as such'. And this first formulation also
makes clear that the category of 'politics as such' carries a special
valence or charge, as a placeholder for the revolutionary transformation of society.

---

14 See 'A Welfare Culture?', one of Mulhern's pivotal essays, which first
appeared in *Radical Philosophy* in 1996, was reprinted in *The Present Lasts a Long
Time: Essays in Cultural Politics*, Cork 1998, and extensively re-used in *Culture/
Metaculture*.
15 Francis Mulhern, *The Moment of 'Scrutiny'*, London 1979, p. 330 (emphases
in the original).

In his subsequent work, Mulhern has broadened and refined this argument but retained its essential structure. Thus, in the Introduction to *Culture/Metaculture* he claims: 'The unifying theme of Parts I and II is the relationship between culture, in its conflicting senses, and the idea of politics . . . [The logic of meta-culture attempts to] resolve the tension of the relationship between culture and politics by dissolving political reason itself.' The specific, and frequently reiterated, charge against the Kulturkritik tradition concerns its alleged contention that 'politics is inherently deficient as a mode of general authority, which can emerge only from the elusive life of the whole, or culture'. And again, as we have already seen, he insists in his most recent restatement that 'culture-as-principle anticipates the end of politics'.[16]

In other words, it is *Mulhern* who, from the outset of his writing career, has insisted that 'culture' and 'politics' have hitherto been locked into this contrastive and mutually excluding relationship, a kind of zero-sum game of public debate. And in so doing, he has always appeared to suggest that politics is, in some sense, the rightful occupant of this public space, with the proponents of 'culture' adopting various strategies to supplant it. All these latter figures have now been brought together as 'the tradition of Kulturkritik', all logically committed to attempting to displace politics. Against this flawed tradition he now proposes an understanding of 'cultural politics' that takes place within, and makes creative use of, the 'discrepancy' between culture and politics. But earlier forms of cultural criticism do not seem to be permitted their own versions of this discrepancy: they are committed to the 'categorial dissolution of politics as such'.

However, if there is a virtue to recognizing and working within 'a tension between culture and politics', then this tension must surely be allowed to work productively in *both* directions: there can be fruitful cultural criticism of politics, just as there can be fruitful political criticism of culture. There can also be exaggerated forms of each, attempting to resolve all cultural questions into 'politics' or all political questions into 'culture'. Mulhern

---

16   Mulhern, *Culture/Metaculture*, pp. xx–xxi, 156, 100.

focuses on this latter deformation, though he precisely does not represent it as an *exaggeration*, but as the ineluctable 'logic' of the appeal to culture itself. All this raises the question of whether, for Mulhern, there can be such a thing as legitimate 'cultural criticism', and that in turn prompts the subordinate historical question of whether there have been 'cultural critics', in the period stretching roughly from Herder to Hoggart, whose work has *not* manifested the defining errors of Kulturkritik. Everything seems, again, to turn on definitions; but one cannot help suspecting that, if any given historical figure wrote in a vein that naturally allowed them to be described as a 'cultural critic', then in terms of Mulhern's conceptual grid they will be bound to manifest the failings of metacultural discourse.

III. 'The Damned Word'[17]

At this point, we need to pause and attend more closely to the senses of the key terms of 'culture' and 'politics' deployed in this argument. Mulhern's handling of 'culture' presupposes and extends the discussion in Raymond Williams's *Culture and Society*. This is, of course, true of most treatments of the topic in Britain now, especially those conceived under the joint stars of left politics and literary studies. In this style of work, Williams's account has been internalized and naturalized to the point where it has ceased to be recognized (as it originally was) as one polemical reinterpretation of a complex story, and has come to be regarded simply as the accepted history of the category of 'culture'. This is not the occasion to take issue with Williams's account in any detail, but it is relevant to call attention to certain of its features, which have become almost invisible.

First, as Williams later took some pride in emphasizing, it was he who selected, arranged and christened the 'culture-and-society

---

17   Cf. Raymond Williams's understandable sigh about 'culture': 'The number of times I've wished that I had never heard of the damned word.' *Politics and Letters: Interviews with New Left Review*, London 1979, p. 154.

tradition': it did not exist as a tradition except as constituted by his argument.[18] Secondly, this tradition is represented as part of the response to a single, cataclysmic social change: the supersession of the older form of society by the 'new civilization' introduced by the Industrial Revolution of the late eighteenth century. Thirdly, what supposedly unites its members is not a shared recognition of belonging, nor a common body of doctrine, nor even a collective use of the term 'culture'. It is, rather, a negative criterion: 'The development of the idea of culture has, throughout, been a criticism of what has been called the bourgeois idea of society.' Fourthly, this new civilization was understood to have been inherently oppressive and inhumane in a way no previous form of society had been; as a result, there was a unique need to create a 'court of appeal' in the form of culture ('over the England of 1821 there had, after all, to be some higher Court of Appeal').[19] Note also the implication here that the politics of the new civilization were assumed to be inadequate for this purpose—a part of the problem rather than any form of remedy.

The result of operating within the conceptual geography of these assumptions about 'culture and society' is that the idea of culture is necessarily seen as something reactive, a primitive critique of 'the bourgeois idea of society' which needs to be superseded by a more sophisticated one—from whose vocabulary the very identification of 'the bourgeois idea of society' is taken. Part of the legacy of Williams's hugely influential book has been to represent any invocation of 'culture' as a call for wholeness and organic unity *by definition*, because the 'reality' that culture was supposed to 'compensate' for was (also by definition, apparently) 'fragmented', 'atomistic', 'disintegrating', and so on.

Of course, it was part of Williams's argument that the notion of culture whose development he claimed to have plotted was insufficient—that it had become 'an abstraction and an absolute'—and that what was required was to rethink the notion of culture-as-a-whole-way-of-life in terms of the ethic of solidarity

---

18   Ibid., p. 99.
19   Williams, *Culture and Society*, pp. 328, 48.

and community, evident in the institutions and achievements of working-class life during this period.[20] But that aspiration, pursued in the long concluding chapter of *Culture and Society*, only casts his predecessors further back into a critically distanced past, and it is this intellectual gesture, it seems to me, that Mulhern—restating some of Williams's historical case, even if going beyond his theoretical conclusion—in effect repeats. In this connexion, it is illuminating to recall that Williams's interviewers in 1979, in urging a wider international perspective than the purely 'English' scope of *Culture and Society*, alluded to the then recently published work of Göran Therborn and summarized the whole European tradition of sociology in terms almost identical to those in which Mulhern now identifies Kulturkritik: 'In one form or another the antidote of classical sociology to the disintegrating forces of industrialism and democracy was always a more organic culture— a coherent order of values capable of conferring a new meaning and unity in society.' The very next reference is to Mann's *Reflections of an Unpolitical Man*, a constant reference point of Mulhern's work right up to the present.[21]

However, there is a sense in which *Culture/Metaculture* builds not so much upon *Culture and Society* itself but upon the criticisms of that work made by Williams's *New Left Review* interviewers in 1979. This is particularly the case with the *political* omissions and inadequacies of that book as the interviewers represented them—the way the book 'appears to exclude the middle term of politics', that it is marked by 'a general depreciation of politics', that 'there does appear to be a virtually systematic depreciation of the actual political dimension of all the figures

---

20   I am puzzled by Mulhern's passing observation that this is a 'questionable' reading of Williams's conclusion ('Beyond Metaculture', above, p. 50). Of course, Williams also distinguished the 'idea of service', but he did not see this as a genuine supersession of 'that version of social relationship which we usually call individualism'. 'The crucial distinction is between alternative ideas of the nature of social relationship', and 'The idea of solidarity is potentially the real basis of society': *Culture and Society*, pp. 325, 332.

21   Williams, *Politics and Letters*, p. 114; cf. Mulhern, *The Present Lasts a Long Time*, pp. 85–6, and *Culture/Metaculture*, pp. 4–7.

whom you are discussing', and so on.[22] But where the *NLR* panel were precisely calling for, as they saw it, the re-introduction of politics as a 'middle term' (that is, between culture and society), Mulhern's latest statement of his case appears to go further and to see any valorization of the critical perspective of culture as entailing the 'systematic depreciation of politics'. The danger then is that Williams becomes an early victim, even if one of the most sympathetically treated, of the intellectual dynamics of the zero-sum game I identified a moment ago.

Senses of Politics

Let me now turn to the other semantic player in this game. The rhetorical pivot around which much of Mulhern's argument turns, both in this exchange and in his work more generally, is a contrast between two senses of 'politics'. When he is discussing Kulturkritik's jeremiads against the failings of contemporary 'civilization', 'politics' appears in the conventional, newspaper's reader's sense—the everyday doings of politicians, parties and parliaments. But when he is indicting that tradition, from his own analytic standpoint, for attempting to 'displace politics' or to 'dissolve political reason itself', something more encompassing and more elevated is in play. 'Politics' here means all that bears on the attempt to order social relations in the light of conceptions of human possibility: it is the continuing activity of trying to refine and give practical effect to such conceptions within a field of conflict. 'Politics is the struggle to determine the totality of social relations in a given space.' Cultural criticism's complaints against current versions of politics in the narrower sense are then held to be part of a broader 'logic' wherein it is attempting to displace politics in the second, larger sense.[23]

---

22 Williams, *Politics and Letters*, pp. 108, 103, 100.

23 'Beyond Metaculture', above, p. 62. It is interesting here to note that Raymond Williams, when pressed by his *NLR* interviewers (of whom Mulhern was of course one) about the 'virtually systematic depreciation' of politics in *Culture and Society*, acknowledged some truth in the charge by saying that when he wrote the book he had 'reached a conclusion that I do not wholly disavow today, although

The structural importance to Mulhern's position of this movement between senses of 'politics' is obliquely confirmed by its
being the occasion for a slight misrepresentation of my argument
in 'Culture Talk':

> Politics, in the language of Collini's critique, is a negative value,
> normally qualified as 'everyday', 'instrumental', 'present-
> driven', or pejoratively associated with 'narrow pragmatism'
> and 'partial or specialized perspectives'. It is the lesser moral
> reality against which culture-as-subject exercises its power of
> general reflection.[24]

A footnote then refers to my article, 'pp. 48–51, *passim*'. Now, it is
of course true that my argument involved appealing to some
conception of the standpoint from which 'cultural criticism' offers
to speak, and that that standpoint involves making a distinction
(perhaps only a preliminary or opportunist distinction: it doesn't
require to be more at this point) between the world of instrumental activity and the world of culture. But what is not true is that I
equate the former with 'politics'. For example, on the first of the
pages cited, I refer to the notion of culture as 'a useful mnemonic
for the kinds of values that those principally engaged in controlling the wealth and power of the world habitually tend to neglect',
and I speak of the effect such appeals to 'culture' can have upon
'those processes that are governed by the need to bring about
proximate instrumental ends'. In so far as any one conventional
term embraces the greater part of such 'instrumental' activity, it is
clearly the 'economic', not the 'political'. Similarly, Mulhern takes
my remark about 'partial or specialized perspectives' as a further

---

I sharply watch myself through it: that there is a kind of politics whose local tactical
modes positively prevent people from seeing what is happening in society—as
distinct from a politics that is based on an understanding of the main lines of force
in society and a choice of sides in the conflict between them. Politics often functions,
not as I think you are using the term, as a conscious struggle or strategy formed by
history and by theory, but as a routine reproduction of controversies or competitive
interests without relation to the basic deep movements of society.' *Politics and
Letters*, p. 103.
24   'Beyond Metaculture', above, p. 62.

pejorative characterization of politics. But in this case, the quoted phrase occurs in my discussion of Raymond Williams's claim that the concept of 'culture' evolved as 'the effort at total qualitative assessment'. I at that point suggest that 'the *generality* of the perspective is the key here', and immediately go on: 'The contrast is with all partial or specialized perspectives.' Throughout my discussion, a familiar set of contrasts is reiterated (it is part of my point that these are long-established pairings, not at all original to me): 'autotelic' versus 'instrumental', 'general' versus 'partial', and so on.

Most of everyday social activity is necessarily and rightly 'instrumental' and 'partial' in these senses. Their opposites, various forms of non-practical creative and reflective activity which, in turn, enable a degree of 'standing back' from instrumentality, are exceptional; and such standing back is, I argue, one of the defining marks of what is usually termed 'cultural criticism'. Clearly, a search for perspectives of greater generality may also inform political activity at its most reflective, and it is neither an explicit nor implicit part of my case here to devalue politics as a 'lesser moral reality'. The thought that the practice of politics may sometimes fall short of the ideal of ordering social relations in the light of conceptions of human possibility, that it may exhibit some of the short-sightedness and narrow calculation characteristic of instrumental activity, and that it may fruitfully be subject to 'criticism', is not to represent politics as a 'negative value'. But all this underlines that it is an important part of Mulhern's argument to represent cultural criticism as unwarrantedly dismissive of 'politics' (conceiving it only in the narrow sense), while reserving for his own position the full recognition of the intellectual reach and human dignity of the activity of 'politics' (in the broad sense). The corresponding danger might appear to be that of asserting a 'political principle' every bit as imperial as the 'cultural principle' he claims to find at the heart of metacultural discourse.

In the end, the ghost at the feast is the notion of a real, or properly serious, 'politics' (in the more general sense) which underwrites Mulhern's criticisms of rival positions. He stigmatizes these positions as being able to offer no more than 'metapolitics'. Even the apparent ubiquity of a form of political commitment in Cultural Studies remains self-frustrating, he argues, because still governed by the logic of metaculture. 'Metacultural discourse', he concludes, damningly, 'is metapolitics.'[25] But so, too, one may retort, is the critique of metacultural discourse in the name of an abstract idea of 'politics'. Indeed, perhaps I may retrieve the truth inexactly expressed in the italicized sentence from 'Culture Talk' quoted above, by now saying that *discourse about metapolitical discourse is still a form of metapolitical discourse*. Metapolitics, one might say, adapting another of Mulhern's dicta about metaculture, urges politics as the necessary, unregarded truth of society, whose curse is the inadequacy of the prevailing forms of general authority.

But metapolitics—to abuse a phrase of Auden's—makes nothing happen. This is not a failing in itself: most intellectual activity is not an attempt to (in the relevant sense) make something happen. The objectionable element comes when intellectuals delude themselves that what they are doing in their intellectual activity is, somehow, 'really' politics. Mulhern is an acute diagnostician of this delusion when discussing some of the recent manifestos for Cultural Studies, but I wonder whether a form of the criticism cannot also be levelled at his own gestures towards 'cultural politics'. The invocation of the *concept* of 'politics', however sophisticated or radical, is not itself politics.

In this context, it also seems legitimate to query the credentials of the position that allows Mulhern to distinguish so confidently between politics and metapolitics. One of his restatements of the case against Kulturkritik is that it proposes, in the name of culture, 'to mediate a symbolic metapolitical resolution of the contradictions of capitalist modernity'. But from my perspective, it appears to be both the strength and the weakness of a broadly Marxist approach to such issues that it can indict other positions for offering no more than such a 'symbolic metapolitical resolution' of these contradictions. The strength lies, of course, in Marxism's strenuously analytical account of the centrality of class conflict,

---

25 Mulhern, *Culture/Metaculture*, p. 157.

and its consequent commitment to political mobilization organized around objectively differentiated relations to the means of production. But the weakness lies in the status of the promised 'resolution' itself, for it is surely now clearer than ever that there is something culpably gestural about Marxism's promise to remake social relations on some other basis and to abolish those economic and social antagonisms that it identifies as having hitherto been the motor of historical change. That claim always relied too heavily on Marx's reworking of Hegel's philosophy of history; and, notoriously, his vision of what kind of society might then succeed capitalism was sketchy in the extreme. In these terms Marxism, too, could be said to offer (no less but also no more than) 'a symbolic metapolitical resolution of the contradictions of capitalist modernity'. Those who find any cogency in this thought will not easily be persuaded that Mulhern is speaking from a position of strength in indicting cultural criticism for falling short of some 'fully political' resolution of these contradictions.

IV. Cultural Criticism vs Cultural Politics

By this point, readers could be forgiven for feeling some frustration that Mulhern and I appear to agree on so much yet to differ on everything. We both insist on the non-identity of culture and politics. We both recognize politics as the important, inescapable, and difficult attempt to determine relations of power in a given space. We both have reservations about the extent to which so many on the left, especially the academic left, now treat questions of cultural identity, variously conceived, as the defining issues of politics. We both believe that those forms of criticism that seek to resolve the problems they diagnose simply by asserting the desirability or inevitability of some kind of harmony are indeed guilty of an evasion of politics. And we both seem drawn to a similar tone or writerly stance in discussing these matters, including a taste for certain kinds of intellectual irony. So, is there, in the end, any real difference between what he chooses to term 'cultural politics' and what I prefer to persist in calling 'cultural criticism'?

I think there is. It turns in part on the issues discussed so far—Mulhern's 'compensatory' notion of culture and the corresponding insistence on the primacy of a certain conception of politics. But perhaps it also turns to some extent upon my understanding of the part to be played in public debate by representatives of imaginative and intellectual activity, and the necessarily disjunctive character, and correspondingly limited effectiveness, of 'criticism'.

I mentioned at the outset of this essay that it still seems to me helpful, for present purposes, to use the term 'culture' in its primary sense of 'artistic and intellectual activities'. Understood thus, 'cultural criticism' signifies the movement from this complex of artistic and intellectual work outward, towards society. Perhaps only 'towards', because such criticism does not usually grapple in any very sustained or detailed way with the perceived defects of that society. After all, to grapple really closely is in the end to *become* politics, as Mulhern emphasizes in respect of particular examples of 'deliberately culturalized politics'.[26] But this is where what I referred to as the necessarily disjunctive character, and correspondingly limited effectiveness, of 'criticism' comes in. Criticism cannot aspire to 'replace' politics, not least because, as criticism, it cannot do what politics requires. Indeed, I do not think that 'cultural criticism' in my sense can or should claim to be terribly effective or influential *as politics*. It issues reminders from time to time, reminders of things not sufficiently taken into account in the prevailing local (and more than local) public discourse; but then its practitioners tend to return to their own preferred preoccupations. Writing, painting, composing, and so on are legitimate, if somewhat rarefied, human activities, and the category to which they belong is not best understood as a form of escape from, or compensation for, the unsatisfactory qualities of (other aspects of) 'reality'. But they are activities that may, from time to time, help prompt the kind of reflections on those other aspects of reality that immersion in those aspects themselves does not so readily tend to foster.

---

26 'Beyond Metaculture', above, p. 65.

Of course, to identify two realms as disjunctive is not to condemn them to an eternity of non-communication. It is surely quite common for a perspective that will eventually be developed into a political critique and, later still, elaborated into a political programme, to have been nourished and partly shaped at an early stage by ideals drawn from 'culture' in this way. The development of the thinking of the young Marx provides one familiar example of this pattern, as notions of self-creation and free activity encountered in the writings of the German Romantics helped stimulate his extraordinary pursuit of explanations of the mechanisms by which the tendentially dominant form of modern society systematically denied these possibilities to its members. In this sense, the *1844 Manuscripts* bears a family resemblance to, say, *Culture and Anarchy*—at times quite a close resemblance, given their common debts to the German Romantics—despite the enormous differences in theoretical ambition, intellectual idiom, mode of address, and so on. Moreover, both works were disparaging of much that counted as 'politics' in the everyday, newspaper reader's sense; yet it would surely seem odd to want to charge either of them with aiming 'to dissolve political reason itself'. In citing Marx and Arnold, I am not proposing either of them as models for contemporary cultural criticism to emulate, but merely indicating some of the ways in which, historically, cultural criticism has had a bearing on what may be conventionally distinguished from it as 'political thought', without attempting illegitimately to supplant the latter.

A Critical Engagement?

Mulhern's response to my earlier version of these claims is one of the few places where he seems to proceed more by assertion than by argument, and this is where our differences may become most explicit. He summarizes my position in the form of an embedded quotation: ' "Disciplined reflection partly grounded in an extensive intellectual and aesthetic inheritance can furnish a place to stand" in "critical engagement" with politics.' He then retorts:

It cannot. In the Arnoldian problematic that governs Collini's reasoning at this point, the first phrase is no more than an elaboration of the second. No other kind of engagement could be critical in the required sense, and the question of a place—a location in the contested order of social value—remains unanswered.[27]

I am not certain I know how to construe these sentences. The first point appears to involve a charge of circular reasoning—Mulhern introduces the section by saying 'the formulations in which he sets out his position are circular'. Presumably, he is suggesting that 'critical engagement' with politics more or less *means* 'disciplined reflection partly grounded in an extensive intellectual and aesthetic inheritance'. This is surely to make the relation between these phrases excessively tight: the kind of 'critical engagement' with politics that, for example, environmentalists or feminists could be said to have may not seem to them to be even partly grounded in an extensive aesthetic inheritance. But even if, for the sake of the argument, one granted some such internal relation between these phrases, I am still not sure that the charge of disabling circularity sticks. Although I do not at all wish to accuse Mulhern of serious or deliberate misquotation at this point, his abbreviation of my sentence does, I think, alter its emphasis a little, and the original makes the non-circularity clearer. What I actually wrote was that the appeal to culture

> does not require the positing of 'culture' as some kind of given or transcendent locus of value; it only requires the presumption that disciplined reflection partly grounded in an extensive intellectual and aesthetic inheritance can furnish a place to stand in attempting to engage critically with the narrow pragmatism (or 'specialism') of any particular political programme.[28]

---

27   Ibid., above, p. 61.
28   'Culture Talk', above, p. 40.

The contrast between 'the extensive intellectual and aesthetic inheritance' and 'the narrow pragmatism . . . of any particular political programme' is surely great enough to avoid circularity: 'critical engagement' with the latter is not coextensive with the former. Nor is this defence weakened by acknowledging, first, that criticism which speaks from a base in such an 'inheritance' may not actually manage to make much of a dent in the certainties of the relevant political programme; and secondly, that of course one could imagine a politics in which this level of critical engagement was constitutive of its own forms of reasoning, but that level of reflectiveness is hardly characteristic of 'political programmes' in general—and, where it is to be found, it may anyway be part of a politics that has drawn with advantage upon earlier forms of cultural criticism.

Mulhern's second point, about 'a location in the contested order of social value', I take to be one about finding an alignment or affiliation within a field of social conflict, where the 'standing' involves standing shoulder to shoulder with some against others. That is an intelligible and indeed familiar notion, but clearly not the sense of 'place to stand' to which I was referring. It looks here as though Mulhern is simply asserting that such a *social* location is the only meaningful sense that could be (or ought to be?) given to that phrase.

The sense, hereabouts in our exchange, that we may each be blundering about in the other's prose, trying to cope with the unfamiliar by reclothing it in more familiar garb, is strengthened by Mulhern's going on to assimilate what I say to the position explored (and criticized) in Marcuse's classic 1937 essay 'The Affirmative Character of Culture'. Mulhern quotes my observation that 'culture' can be seen as

> an allusion to the bearing which that kind of disinterested or autotelic exploration of human possibility, characteristically (but not exclusively) pursued in artistic and intellectual activity, can have upon those processes that are governed by the need to bring about proximate instrumental ends.

He then comments that this 'simply assumes what it needs to establish. The word "characteristically" is an ideological wand.'[29] I am particularly puzzled by this last phrase. Presumably, Mulhern would agree that such exploration *is* pursued in artistic and intellectual activity, so perhaps he is suggesting that my statement exaggerates this truth or thereby obscures another more important one. But the metaphor of the wand suggests more than this: it suggests a shady or unconvincing attempt to transform something into something else. Perhaps the objection to 'characteristically' is that it functions to turn what is really the activity of politics (in Mulhern's most ambitious sense) into the activity of culture. But that reading, I have to say, 'simply assumes what it needs to establish'. Nor am I cowed by the thought that 'Marcuse might have seized on it [my use of "characteristically"] to illustrate the transmutation of the historical generality of art and ideas into a transcendent value whose content is its negation of the realm of interests'. Marcuse might indeed have done so; but that, in my view, would have been for him merely to have extended the intellectual high-handedness of his original characterization of 'the affirmative character of culture'. For it would be, first, to have assumed too complete and contrastive a distinction between 'culture' and 'society' (despite my qualification 'characteristically but not exclusively'); second, it would have been yet again to work with an excessively functionalist analysis of culture, which sees it as some form of 'compensation' for the injustices of the prevailing social order; and third, it would be to assign criticism of instrumental activity to 'another world', to require it to inhabit a 'transcendental' realm. Working with the categories derived from a Marxist recasting of the broader German Idealist tradition of philosophy and social theory, Marcuse was able to make each of these claims in its positive form seem like a necessary conceptual truth, but it is not a necessary truth that everyone who writes about culture has to work within those categories.

---

29   'Beyond Metaculture', above, p. 62.

V. Intellectuals and Their Work

Perhaps part of the emerging pattern of differences between Mulhern and myself on these issues can be traced back to contrasting attitudes to the role of intellectuals. Mulhern has long objected to what he identifies as the assertion of the claims of a 'new priesthood' implicit in the tradition of cultural criticism, since it presumes a notion of culture as the possession of the cultivated few, 'by definition inaccessible to the great majority'. I believe myself to be no more in favour of a 'new priesthood' than Mulhern (though he may still think this is the 'logic' of my position), but I also believe that the activity of cultural criticism need not entail any such notion. As I have indicated, it seems to me a drawback of his expanded category of Kulturkritik that it makes such caste-consciousness inescapable. Thus, a given writer's 'personal democratic convictions do not cancel the fact' that in writing in this vein he or she is 'simply updating the claims' of what, speaking of Karl Mannheim in 1988, Mulhern called 'a pseudo-aristocratic authoritarian liberalism'. Or as he puts it in his most recent piece: 'That superordination of culture-as-principle, and of an intellectual corps privy to its meaning, can only be authoritarian, in final effect, even where the associated social aspiration is benign and progressive.'[30]

The dangers of talking too freely of the 'logic' of an ascribed intellectual position surely become evident here. Describing a 'benign and progressive' position as 'authoritarian, in final effect' seems to me all too reminiscent of that mid-twentieth-century communist jargon in which positions could be dismissed as 'objectively fascist' no matter what their ostensible political orientation. 'Final' effect seems to presuppose knowledge of a process and its outcome that is beyond any epistemology legitimately available to the intellectual historian.

In this vein, Mulhern sees a form of 'humanism' at work here: 'Humanism and its distinctive guardian—the intellectual, the

---

30   Mulhern, *The Present Lasts a Long Time*, pp. 87–8; 'Beyond Metaculture', above, p. 51.

Arnoldian "best self" of an "ordinary" world—are living, more vigorously and more variously than many of us would like to think.'[31] I, predictably, do not find 'humanism', used in this sense, a very helpful label, and I certainly see no reason to tie the inescapable sociological category of 'the intellectual' to a dubious and unappealingly dated notion of the Arnoldian 'best self'. But meta-cultural discourse is represented as the characteristic or occupational failing of intellectuals, precisely because it attempts to assert the primacy of their defining activities. A kind of corporatism is made to appear inescapable, therefore: speaking in the name of culture is inherently 'authoritarian', an assertion of the esoteric knowledge possessed by the privileged few, whereas speaking in the name of 'politics' allows an implication of some kind of democratic labour, subserving the interests of others.

Behind Mulhern's various strictures on the 'elitist' and 'pseudo-aristocratic' failings of past cultural critics there lies, it seems to me, not just a theoretical antipathy but a more personal unease with the fact of *being* an intellectual. After all, we need to ask how we should understand the activity of writing books and essays about the relation of culture and politics—in other words, the activity that Mulhern himself is engaged in. For there can be no question but that he is writing as an intellectual: drawing upon the kind of disciplined engagement with history, literature and philosophy that has been facilitated by his education and employment, he aspires to persuade his readers to adopt his way of thinking about these large issues. The proponent of 'cultural politics', no less than that of 'cultural criticism', speaks from a more general perspective than the one currently—perhaps only temporarily—occupied by those whom they are both trying to persuade.

This is not a reprehensibly 'elitist' conception of the role of the intellectual. It is an inevitable feature of the form taken by intellectual labour, in so far as it participates in public debate. There is no sense, therefore, in which to speak from the perspective of 'culture' is inherently authoritarian while to speak from that of

---

31   Mulhern, *The Present Lasts a Long Time*, p. 92; cf. Mulhern, *Culture/ Metaculture*, pp. xvi–xvii, 34–5.

'politics' is inherently democratic or egalitarian. Obviously the manner in which either is done may be more or less democratic in any given instance—as may what Mulhern calls the 'associated social aspiration'. Nonetheless, the structural position of drawing upon certain intellectual or cultural advantages in order to try to persuade others to understand the world (or some bit of it) in the recommended way is the same, in both cases. The fact that some cultural critics may have made unwarranted assumptions about a kind of caste superiority does not mean that attempts to bring the perspective of culture to bear on the common discussion of common problems must always be dismissed as 'elitist', even assuming that that much-misused word still retains any dismissive force. Conversely, the fact that the ideal to which Mulhern ultimately looks forward is one in which all may participate in the 'general labour' of pondering 'human possibility' and its translation into social practice does not mean that, in recommending this conception *now*, he escapes the necessarily asymmetrical relations of intellectuals and publics.

But (to avoid misunderstanding) I should declare still more emphatically that I do not endorse the condescension and cultural pessimism of those inter-war cultural critics whom Mulhern so effectively criticizes. Cultural criticism does not have to assume an authoritarian relation between a priesthood of cultivated adepts and a merely passive mass of the uninstructed. Equally, it does not require the disparagement of a set of phenomena selectively grouped as 'modernity', nor the assumption of a fall from some previously better or more 'organic' state. But nor, by the same token, does it *have* to aim at the displacement or supersession of politics: only at critically supplementing it. Speaking about broadly political matters from a broadly cultural perspective is both legitimate and likely to be of limited effect. It is only one among the valuable forms of public debate, and by no means always the most important one.

In the perorations to both his book and his subsequent article, Mulhern celebrates the 'discrepancy' between culture and politics as a space of creative possibility. Expressed in those terms, his case might seem bound to win one's enthusiastic support. But, as I have tried to show, the whole critical machinery at work in his category of 'metacultural discourse' presumes that the sphere of public determination of the pattern of social relations as a whole is to be regarded as properly, and exclusively, the domain of 'politics'. Culture enters it as an intruder; indeed, the sphere itself is characterized in such a way that culture can only figure as an illegitimate usurper, always attended by a train of discredited intellectual gestures and dubious political aspirations. Mulhern concludes his most recent restatement by saying that socialists may ponder the precedents of recent forms or episodes of cultural politics 'as they face their own unknowns, chief among them the shapes of an adequate—imaginative and capable—contemporary politics'. I warm to the pluralism of 'shapes' while in the same movement bridling at the drama of 'chief'. Perhaps that movement encapsulates my response to Mulhern's case more generally. Perhaps the differences between us can be crystallized by my wanting to say that, for all the manifold virtues of *Culture/Metaculture* in particular and Mulhern's writings on this theme in general, they still leave us facing another quite important unknown: the shapes of an adequate—imaginative and capable—contemporary cultural criticism.

5

FRANCIS MULHERN

The Logic of Cultural Criticism

Stefan Collini now gives free expression to the concern that was already evident in his first response to *Metaculture*. If the historical category of Kulturkritik and my unorthodox use of it have been prominent in the exchange to date, this is in large part because it is overdetermined by issues whose charge is contemporary and prospective. 'Defending Cultural Criticism' is Collini's title, not 'leave it to the historians'. Of course, criticism and history cannot be simply partitioned in this case. Collini insists with more than conventional force on the continuity between them, and with reason. Nevertheless, I will say nothing more about historic Kulturkritik, except in passing. Neither of us is ready to concede, and others will weigh the arguments for themselves.

That Collini really is engaged in a defence is beyond doubt. But what is the substance of the position he wishes to defend? My purpose here is to attempt an outline of his cultural criticism, as it emerges in response to *Metaculture* and in a selection of other relevant writings from the past fifteen years. It will be necessary to tread lightly. Having begun his scholarly career as an intellectual historian in the contextualist style of Quentin Skinner and his collaborators, Collini has gone on to develop a recognizably literary approach still further at variance with the textbook histories of thought.[1] He has

---

1 His first book, *Liberalism and Sociology: L. T. Hobhouse and Political Argument in England 1880–1914*, Cambridge 1979, acknowledged a debt to Skinner. *Arnold*, Oxford 1988, marks a shift in treatment, confirmed a few years later in *Public Moralists*.

little sympathy with those who expect or impute 'doctrine' or 'system' or 'theory' in the thinkers he studies, and even modest 'views' can be put in their place, which is between ironizing quotation marks.[2] Anyone approaching his own writing in that spirit is open to the charge of intellectual crassness. However, he has given some headwords as preliminary guidance: culture, politics, intellectuals. Others will emerge in the course of discussion.

I. Thinking Cultural Criticism

Collini begins by relieving the phrase 'cultural criticism' of its everyday ambiguity. It is not, or not only, criticism of culture. Culture is what animates and orients the critical practice, whose object is society or, better, 'prevailing public discourse'. This is culture as 'artistic and intellectual activities'—not the only meaning of the term, he agrees, but, as Raymond Williams recognized, the 'primary' one. The criticism it underwrites is politically modest in ambition and effect, not driven as metacultural discourse supposedly is, and certainly not fated to reactionary conclusions. 'Distance', 'reflectiveness' and generality are its defining critical qualities. Its touchstones can be found in T. S. Eliot, but also in Matthew Arnold before him, in George Orwell and later in Richard Hoggart 'and so on'. This is recognizable as a self-description (except in its evocation of Eliot, whom I for one would not have thought to associate with Collini's critical journalism). What is less clear, however, is its logic.

---

2   Collini, *Arnold*, pp. viii, 3; see also *Public Moralists*, p. 3. For his own account of the context of his work in the later 1970s and 80s, see the 'General Introduction', in Stefan Collini, Richard Whatmore and Brian Young, eds, *Economy, Polity and Society: British Intellectual History 1750–1950*, Cambridge 2000, pp. 1–21. This is one of a pair of volumes marking the retirement of Collini's senior collaborators John Burrow and Donald Winch.

The Elusive Value of Culture

Collini emphasizes the semantic difficulty of 'culture': this was the opening note of 'Culture Talk', and he strikes it again in his second essay. But the difficulty is not simply semantic, and it cannot be resolved, even temporarily, by a self-aware, negotiated protocol of usage of the kind he now sets out. For if the restrictive meaning of culture is in one respect shared, as familiar currency, in another it is a site of inescapable contention. It is possible to reach a working agreement about the kinds of thing that count as instances of 'culture' in his sense; there will be boundary disputes, but none so fierce as to unmake the field as such. However, the empirical reference of the term is overdetermined by its disputed conceptual significance. The 'other meanings' of culture, which Collini peaceably sets aside for other occasions, inhabit its 'narrower sense', as parties to a conceptual antagonism now inherent in it.

Two constructions of this same 'sense' are especially pertinent. In the first, culture marks a convergence of positive values in opposition to non-culture, the prevailing order of good sense. This, in the language of *Metaculture*, is culture as principle. In the second, associated with Williams and cultural studies, the narrow empirical reference survives alongside the wider one, but under a different concept. The same material is now thought differently, understood as a specific historical formation of values and practices, a 'high' register within the social relations of meaning as a whole. Literature and philosophy are not simply dissolved into 'a whole way of life', a phrasing that Williams borrowed from Eliot in his early formulations of his own distinct object of inquiry, which was '*the relations between elements* in a whole way of life'.[3] Even where they are set aside in favour of the unexplored world of popular pleasures and identifications, as they were, with deforming intellectual consequences, in the new routines of cultural studies, they persist as aspects of a reconstructed object, the social relations of meaning as a whole. Were it not so, the new concept of culture would simply invert the dualism of the old, foreclosing

---

3 Williams, *Culture and Society*, pp. 11–12, emphasis added.

its own theoretical implications, which reach into every corner of empirical 'culture'. The old 'sense' of culture is an aspect of the historical object of the new one, which is what Yuri Lotman termed 'the semiosphere' (a coinage that has the signal advantage of not being that damned word).[4] Reiterated uncritically, it is too much for the purposes of Collini's cultural criticism, just as the second, properly understood, is too little.

Culture in the first case is too much in that it presupposes a subject that can occupy that site of convergence, speaking from and to a general interest. Not welcoming the philosophical burden of that logic, Collini dismisses its embodiment, Arnold's 'best self', as 'dubious and unappealingly dated', and that, apparently, is that. The second construction accords more closely with his intramundane appreciation of culture and society, but not in a way that furthers the project of cultural criticism. For in this case, art and ideas take shape and direction in the same divided historical world of sense that frames 'prevailing public discourse'—to which, indeed, they bring their distinctive varieties of texture and finish. 'Distance' can be more than conventional, yet still measurable within the space of the ideological dominant. He will not have forgotten Williams's analysis of the English industrial novel, in which strong, eloquent witness to the reality of working-class suffering coexisted, imaginatively, with an ungovernable fear of mass irrationality.[5] Literature is no less prone to such disturbance of vision when it turns 'reflective' in the stronger sense, and examines the relationship between its own genus, culture, and society. For example, it would be difficult not to read Hardy's *Jude the Obscure* for what, in one clear sense, it is: a critique, in tragic mode, of the prevailing social order of culture. Yet it is not easy to overlook the ambiguity of its truncated biblical motto, which puts learning itself in question: 'the letter killeth'.[6] Untimely death has been a standard outcome in the English 'condition of culture'

---

4   Yuri M. Lotman, *Universe of the Mind: A Semiotic Theory of Culture*, London 1990, pp. 123–214.

5   Williams, *Culture and Society*, Part I, Chapter 5.

6   2 Corinthians 3. The full declaration is 'The letter killeth, but the spirit giveth life'.

novel, figuring a narrative judgement on those characters who think to honour culture, or aspire to it, or think to impart it, or simply inherit it. Reardon in *New Grub Street*, Bast in *Howards End*, Melinda and her family in *A Judgement in Stone* are, like Jude and Sue in Hardy's novel, among the slightly ridiculous victims of culture's ambivalent relationship to its best self.[7]

The doubled reflectivity of the critic—intellectual activity directed to the arts—offers further adverse testimony, suggesting that distance is too purely formal a criterion to assist the inevitably substantive choices entailed in any criticism of society. Eliot took his critical distance from post-war Britain, with explicitly reactionary intent. Hoggart also measured a distance, from the vantage-point of culture 'in the narrow sense', but made an antithetical reading of present dangers and possibilities. His critique of cultural commerce did not extend to the capitalist property relation itself, or to the paternalism of official cultural policy. Williams's crucial initiative, following on from his critical reflection on 'the idea of culture', was to bring both into theoretical view as the matrix of contemporary cultural organization, and to urge a socialist alternative based on a revised theoretical account of culture. There is a *reductio ad absurdum* in these comparisons. Here are three reflective, critically distant contributions to post-war discussion of culture and society. They all meet Collini's minimum criteria for cultural criticism, and they are mutually incompatible. Yet it is difficult to see how a critic equipped only with the developed aptitudes that Collini specifies could set about discriminating among them—how 'culture', so reduced, could energize and direct a critique.

The Status of Politics

Having saved culture by moderating its agonistic theoretical content, Collini then restores proportion to the question of politics in a counterpart stroke, discovering in my generic references

---

7   George Gissing, 1891; E. M. Forster, 1910; Ruth Rendell, 1977; Hardy, 1896.

to 'politics' not the single meaning I emphatically intend, but two. Again, they come broad and narrow. When I discuss 'Kulturkritik's jeremiads against the failings of contemporary "civilization",' he writes, '"politics" appears in the conventional, newspaper reader's sense'. But when I 'indict that tradition . . . for attempting to "displace politics" or to "dissolve political reason itself", something more encompassing and more elevated is in play'[8]—in my own words, politics as 'the struggle to determine the totality of social relations in a given space'. This perceived duality is what used to be called a strong misreading— and one that courts danger just at the point where it appeals to the authority of common experience, in the figure of the newspaper reader.

It must have been difficult for a curious reader of the European press, between the Armistice and the crash of 1929, to rest for long with distinctions of the kind that Collini has in mind. Revolution and counterrevolution, or the expectation of such outcomes, civil war, nation-building and constitution-making were among the familiar extremities of the decade, toning the experience of public affairs even in the less troubled polities of the continent. The cultural critics, who surely counted among the more attentive readers of the time, made no such distinction. Mann rejected politics *tout court* as un-German; Mannheim's intellectual strategy was pitched against 'the party schools' of the far left and right. Leavis's sense of the final triviality of politics found expression not so much in his disdain for the Westminster everyday as in his refusal of communism, which was the occasion for some of his most trenchant programmatic declarations. For Benda and Ortega, the state of journalism was itself a prime symptom of politically conditioned crisis, evidenced most graphically in the proliferation of agitational sheets that find no buyers, only sellers.[9] In every

---

8 'Defending Cultural Criticism', above, p. 83 (grammar modified for context).

9 Joseph Roth: 'On Potsdamer Platz, a little forest of papers has been planted . . . You hear the repetitive *hack-hack-hack* of the nationalist woodpecker. But these newspapers find only sellers. I am their sole buyer.' 'Election Campaign in Berlin' [1924], in *What I Saw: Reports from Berlin 1920–1933*, trans. Michael Hofmann, London 2003, p. 192.

case, the cause of alarm was 'encompassing', and 'elevated' indeed, if only in the scale of cultural perversion.

The appeal to the newspaper reader's sense of politics is historically parochial—and perhaps not even that, in so far as it corresponds little better to the domestic experience of the past quarter-century. In my first response to Collini, I distinguished between 'maintenance' and 'transformation' as the basic modes of political practice. It is easy to see how this formula might be read as shadowing the distinction he now finds in *Metaculture*. That reading would be mistaken. The two modes are not simple alternatives or complements. They can cooperate so closely as to differ only as aspects of a single strategy—as they have in the governance of capitalism in Britain since 1979. The well-being of capital and the state was the great, simple principle of Conservative strategy in the 1980s and beyond, just as, in modified form, it is Labour's today. It is the basic sense of 'maintenance' in bourgeois politics. Yet the work of maintenance, in the Thatcher years, took the form of a sequence of departures, initiatives in a concerted class struggle from above that opened a new period in Britain's contemporary history. Unions were cornered and attacked, public assets sold off, social welfare reprogrammed for failure; money was set free and, even as inequality and relative poverty deepened, everyday experience was subjected to new intensities of commodification. Much of this appeared implausible in prospectus, a dream of policy doctrinaires and their vengeful patron. Yet it was achieved, and has now been normalized, both at home and internationally, where it figures as a pioneering example of the new model capitalism. The newspaper readers of recent decades have had an exemplary education in the visionary politics of capital.

Of course, it is possible to grant these arguments and still resist the idea that politics has a claim to final authority in social relations. There are obvious reasons for doing so. The goals of political activity normally lie outside politics, which in that sense cannot claim finality. Political practice has its own necessary disciplines, arising from its agonistic structure, and a campaigning demand is no substitute for the modes of engagement associated with culture—unless, of course, as Collini might say, for 'the mind that

can only think in terms of "positions" '.[10] He is speaking here on
behalf of Arnold rather than himself, but not—if the free indirect
style allows a confident reading—at any significant distance from
the general judgement he reports. It is worth pausing for a moment.
The logic of the half-stated contrast between positional and
another, more adequate kind of thinking is defensively forced. The
modifier 'only' works to marginalize a third possibility, which is
that neither kind is adequate for all relevant purposes. Arnold's
belief in the 'irrigating' value of criticism in public affairs is in
general terms unexceptionable. But this prickly statement of
contrasts appeals to the bolder idea that positional thinking,
which politics entails, is intrinsically wanting, even where it is inescapable; that the cast of mind associated with criticism is intrinsically preferable. Other passages in Collini's study lend credence to
this reading. Arnold's 'deep intellectual affinity' with Platonism
'suggests what might be described as the "anti-political" character
of his thought', he writes.[11] At another moment, he speaks with
unmistakable warmth of 'that kind of literary criticism which is
also cultural criticism and thus . . . a sort of informal political
theory'.[12] The closing phrase is a winningly modest description of
a work—*Culture and Anarchy*—that looked towards an ideal
union of culture and the state.

A bourgeois state, it is pertinent to add; not in a spirit of heroic
retrospection, but because bourgeois society defined Arnold's
imaginative horizon, for all his criticism of it, and quite naturally
shaped his evaluation of political possibility—his sense of what,
in the end, it might be worth. His contemporary Marx saw in the
same society the conditions of a qualitatively superior collective
life beyond it, to be achieved by political means. The difference of
historical perspective is fundamental. For the communist Marx,
the very idea of politics exercised a power of moral attraction that
would have been incongruous for Arnold, the disinterested 'Liberal
of the future'. Collini is not Arnold. He makes a point of

---

10   Collini, *Arnold*, p. 9.
11   Ibid., p. 91.
12   Ibid., p. 67.

informing his readers that his identification with his subject is less strong than it appears to be. Yet it may be that in this regard they are not far apart.

Intellectuals, or Algebra

Overlooking what appears to be a real difference between us, a difference of political evaluation about which there is little to be done, Collini fastens on an imagined one. 'Behind [my] various strictures on the "elitist" and "pseudo-aristocratic" failings of past cultural critics there lies . . . not just a theoretical antipathy but a more personal unease with the fact of *being* an intellectual.' Coming from a critic so keen-eyed and unsparing in his pursuit of the anti-intellectualism of intellectuals, this is a daunting suggestion—or would be, if there were grounds for it. But there are none. Collini is chasing a shadow. What he has to say about the cultural division of labour and its tenacious real effects, about the 'necessarily asymmetrical relations of intellectuals and publics', is uncontroversial—and familiar, with all due qualifications made, from Gramsci and Sartre, among others.

He is right too to insist that the habitus and practice of 'the intellectual' as classically figured—the assumption of public responsibility without benefit of office—need not be 'elitist', though mistaken if he imagines that this resolves the difficulty before us. The question implicit in my 'Intellectual Corporatism and Socialism', a short text from the late 1980s that Collini puts to use at this stage in his argument, concerned the conditions of the 'intellectual' claim, and its moral substance.[13] Corporatist traditions of intellectual self-projection have offered one kind of validation: intellectuals are in principle a cohesive social group, bonded morally in a commitment to universals by virtue of which

---

13 Mulhern, 'Intellectual Corporatism and Socialism: The Twenties and After', in *The Present Lasts a Long Time*, pp. 85–92. See now Francis Mulhern, *Into the Mêlée*, the essay now borrowing the title of the whole collection, London and New York 2024.

they pass judgement on the world. The challenge facing any reasoned—rather than merely declared—version of this general position is to elucidate the social grounding of the universals and to explain, in non-moralistic and non-tautological terms, why, as the empirical record shows, most intellectuals are not, and never have been, 'intellectuals'. The schematic alternative to corporatism is to accept the record as indicating the truth of the matter, which is that the characteristic practice of intellectuals is one modality of intervention among others in the contested field of social relations, rather than a distinctive allegiance within it. However hesitantly, with however much self-monitoring, intellectuals make their choices from a range of historical possibilities that they share with everyone.

Corporatism is not an option for Collini. He shrugs off the association with Arnold's moral-psychological notion of the best self, which would at least support an appeal to universals, and is stung by my use of the term 'authoritarian', in which, it may be, he mistakenly senses a demagogic suggestion of epaulettes and riding boots. Yet it seems unlikely that he would settle for the second position, which grants the customary generic figure of 'the intellectual' rather less status than he reserves for it in his own anti-heroic formulation. And there, if anywhere, lies a cause of my unease, which is impersonal and theoretical. If intellectual practice is really so modestly specified, after all, what position can it sustain? This reduced idea of the intellectual, like the abstract 'perspective of culture' with which he now very plausibly associates it, is a piece of algebra: y to the other's x, it is a cipher awaiting its substantive critical value.

II. Doing Cultural Criticism

But perhaps this smacks too much of theory, views, positions, all the effigies of thinking against which Collini the historian has repeatedly warned his audience. At such moments, he echoes those parts of *Culture and Society* where the effort of thinking appears to be privileged over the determinate sense of what is thought. Yet Williams's unambiguous object was the formation of a contemporary discourse. Not an autonomous exercise in historical inquiry or a survey, his book was for a time planned alternatively, as a systematic reconstruction and critique, whose pilot version had appeared as 'The Idea of Culture'.[14] Collini's studies in nineteenth-century and later liberalism, which made up a good part of his specialist writing in the 1980s, share historical personnel with Williams—notably Mill and Arnold—but little else, in theme, treatment or purpose. Whereas Williams attended nearly exclusively to texts and their arguments, Collini has come to emphasize the material and moral phenomena of what he calls 'voice'. Utterance rather than statement takes priority in his analyses, which are striking equally for their attention to the conditions of intellectual practice and their confirmed sense of what finally matters in thought.

The Voice of Thought

'Voice' is a notation for the communicative event as a whole, including the determinate social-cultural relations between writers and readerships, and the pattern of constraint and opportunity inscribed in a given form of communication, which are co-constitutive of a text and its meaning. Collini's reconstruction of 'the world of the Victorian intellectual', with its accounts of incomes, career paths, publishing opportunities and institutional circuits—including a brilliant evocation of the London Athenaeum in the 1850s and 60s—shows how much is lost in any history of mere 'ideas'. In its associated meaning, 'voice' directs us to persons, underpinning a distinctive ordering of priorities in the evaluation of thought. The voice of a text is realized in its 'preferred register and habitual strategies'. As the metaphor suggests, it identifies a writer rather than a genre, and what it communicates, beyond the paraphrasable ideas, is a sensibility. Collini's interest in voice is not only an enriching development in the historical

---

14 Raymond Williams, 'The Idea of Culture', *Essays in Criticism* 1, 1953, pp. 239–66.

understanding of thought; it defines a committed moral stance.
Introducing his monograph on Arnold, he writes:

> Rather than providing a comprehensive summary of [his]
> 'views', I have throughout concentrated on characterizing the
> tone and temper of his mind and the distinctive style in which it
> expressed itself . . . [It] is on account of the qualities embodied
> in his elusive but recognizable literary 'voice', rather than of any
> body of 'doctrine', that he continues to be such rewarding
> company for us.[15]

Opening *Public Moralists*, he summarizes his topic as 'the development of English moral and cultural attitudes, and their bearing
on political argument' across his chosen span, and then sets out
the more strenuous implication of the morality of voice: 'Our
understanding of this aspect of our history, and still more the
manner and tone in which we write about it, are consequential,
albeit in a limited way for our sense of identity and conduct in the
present.'[16]

Manner, tone, identity, conduct and, elsewhere, again in relation to Arnold, 'spirit', which Collini elaborates as 'a cast of mind,
but of more than mind—a temper, a way, at once emotional, intellectual and psychological, of possessing one's experience and
conducting one's life'.[17] So the algebraic series continues, but now
with the unmistakable suggestion that cultural criticism is the
public illustration of essentially personal dispositions.

Criticism as Portraiture

Collini dislodges ideas from their common-sense status as the first
test of intellectual *virtù*. The subjective conditions of good judgement are not given in the concepts it deploys—a moral conviction
with a strong practical corollary in his writing, which, as he says

---

15 Collini, *Arnold*, p. viii.
16 Collini, *Public Moralists*, p. 1.
17 Collini, *Arnold*, p. 5.

himself, tends spontaneously towards the essayistic. His rhetoric, neither aspiring to system nor valuing it in others, is one of occa-sions, which are given by 'culturally pre-formed objects' and the avowedly personal engagements they permit or demand.[18] The objects he chooses, and the qualities he brings to his encounters with them, suggest a further specification of his work. All but two of the sixteen essays in *English Pasts*, the book that best represents his current intellectual practice, were developed from reviews, and of the works reviewed some two-thirds are biographies, memoirs, edited correspondence or institutional studies.[19] To these he brings his considerable powers of observation and empathy, and a gift of mockery to complement that of appreciation. Collini is a natural in the form he practises to such arresting effect, the intel-lectual portrait.

Collini's portraiture is a strong option, integrating ideas with a personality and a life, and thus favouring an order of treatment that does not lend itself to critical reconstruction of the thought. In this way, his practice honours its unargued premise, which, notwithstanding its specific role in disagreements about historical method, has a recognizable antecedent in one of the central commonplaces of literary-liberal culture in the twentieth century: the responsibility of 'literature' and its attendant values in the face of 'ideology'. Literature, in this scheme, is to public discourse what the individual person is to the social order, the limit of clas-sifying presumption. In England in the early twentieth century, this was the shared belief of the Bloomsbury circle: when they protested that they were not the 'Group' as which they became notorious, but merely 'friends', they spoke no more than their ideological truth. That truth passed into general intellectual currency after the Second World War, becoming a topic of literary journalism and not least, today, of the public conversation to which Collini has devoted his cultural criticism.

---

18 Theodor W. Adorno, 'The Essay as Form', in *Notes to Literature*, vol. 1, New York 1991, pp. 3–23.
19 Collini, *English Pasts*.

Tone and Other Cruces

If the idea of portraiture seems to define Collini's characteristic relation to his subjects, the model of conversation, which he sees and admires in Arnold's essays, accounts for his form of address, the writer–reader relations he works towards in his prose. Portraits are of persons; conversations engage persons on terms of relative familiarity, favouring shared over contested values. Conversational portraiture, as criticism, is a variety of performance art with few more accomplished exponents than Stefan Collini. While no single instance can be taken as definitive, there is particular interest in an essay prompted by a book on George Orwell and billed by the *London Review of Books* as 'Christopher Hitchens, Englishman'.[20]

Hitchens rather than Orwell is indeed the subject, and Collini's theme and treatment are alike well caught in his title, '"No Bullshit" Bullshit'. This is an essay about a posture and a certain English intellectual sensibility. Thus, Collini does not dwell for long on the aporia of contrarianism, or 'the animating illusion' that there is never moral strength in numbers, or the romanticism of self-proclaimed 'independence'. His only reference to Hitchens's support for Bush's wars of aggression is the glancing comment that 'too irritable an aversion from one's self-righteously "radical" associates can lead one into some very unlovely company'. The wording of this caution eases readers past the political crisis to which it alludes and into the heart of things, the matter of 'tone' in English culture. Collini writes perceptively about Hitchens's swelling Englishness, and with proper candour, noting the moments of bristling anti-intellectualism and nativist prejudice. He also notes a certain machismo, which he associates with a fixation on public-school experience (though not, as also seems possible, with the hard-boiled school of journalism).

But what is most striking in this essay is its hyperbolic re-enactment, in its own textual space, of the sensibility it lays open for critical inspection. Pugilistic images recur throughout

---

20   Stefan Collini, '"No Bullshit" Bullshit', *London Review of Books*, 23 January 2003.

(including a highly specialized reference to 'watching an old video of a one-sided boxing match'). In a related trope, Hitchens is squared off against two other 'master' reviewers, Martin Amis and Frank Kermode—'a tough poker table to ask anyone to sit at', it seems. Other elements of the rhetoric are distinctly English. Hitchens gives Orwell's detractors a 'duffing-up', and Raymond Williams 'is taken behind the bike shed for a particularly nasty going-over'. Collini speaks fluent BikeShed. 'No one can accuse [Hitchens] of only picking on boys his own size', or of correct relations with 'fags and booze', he reports. 'Yikes!' he exclaims at one juncture, in noisy homage to the public-school novels of his boyhood.

No doubt this is high-spirited irony, in a writer who values high spirits and irony alike. The closing judgement, though witty, is grave enough. Yet irony is ambiguous as a resource for criticism. Just as it unsettles what it appears to maintain, so, in another regard, it spares what it shows to be vulnerable. The irony of irony is that its critical power of displacement remains mere potential while it persists, taking effect only when it stops. But Collini's last word, in keeping with the rhetoric of the essay as a whole, is Hitchens's own: 'bullshit', a vulgarism that illustrates as well as any the phatic, bonding function of language and the adaptive, convivial face of irony.

The idea of 'company' is important to Collini (it has appeared twice already, and will appear again), and his rhetoric serves it faithfully, articulating critical judgement in a shared cultural code that continues to be valued as such. In a brilliantly executed closing paragraph, he pictures Hitchens, returned from a day of horse and hounds, sitting in a pub with Kingsley Amis, Philip Larkin and Robert Conquest, among 'other red-coated, red-faced riders increasingly comfortable in their prejudices and their Englishness'. He continues: 'They would be good company, up to a point, but their brand of saloon-bar frivolity is only a quick sharpener away from philistinism, and I would be sorry to think of one of the essayists I have most enjoyed reading in recent decades turning into a no-two-ways-about-it-let's-face-it bore. I just hope he doesn't go on one hunt too many and find himself, as twilight gathers and the fields fall silent, lying face down in his own bullshit.'

The conceit is an old English Christmas card morphed into caricature. But Collini is not Steve Bell, and his tone, not hostile, is that of saddened reproof. The burden of his judgement remains inexplicit—'elusive', as he would say of Arnold, or perhaps just not fully public in the expected way. The tension in the passage is that of a bond strained but unbroken. This is criticism as home truths.

Home Truths

Home truths have force but little scope. As expressions of crisis in an inescapable relationship, they cannot be ignored, however little truth they actually contain. But for the same reason, their goal is correction, nothing more. They illustrate the limitations of reflexivity strictly understood, and make too modest a template for criticism. The social relations of capitalism are not inescapable, as some at least of the resources termed 'cultural' survive to remind us; the possibility of transformation has not disappeared from history. What Collini makes of this proposition I cannot say. It seems clear, however, that he is little moved by the thought that specifically political contentions might mediate choices of fundamental and positive human significance, and it would be surprising if this strategic hesitation had no bearing on his sense of critical stakes. The terms of evaluation that he brings to public discourse are scarcely political, even where politics is the matter in hand, and not 'cultural' either, in any telling sense: their common denominator is their association with the private sphere. Ideas count for less than the voices that circulate them and the sensibilities that vary their texture. Conversation is a model of public discourse. Cultural and political relationships that cannot be reduced to inter-personal terms are nevertheless appraised for their quality as company. It was one of Hitchens's imagined company, Philip Larkin, who wrote that 'home' begins as 'a joyous shot at how things ought to be'.[21] Cultural criticism, as Collini voices it, shares something of

---

21   Philip Larkin, 'Home Is So Sad' [1958], in *Collected Poems*, London 1988, p. 119.

that indoor utopianism, making a complementary investment in the moral example of friends at table. His moralist is a private face in a public place. It is as though public discourse must learn from a certain kind of commensality—intelligent, decent, and always essentially intimate, even when the talk is of collective crises. What is disavowed here—known, indubitably, yet somehow not consistently imagined—is the specifically social reality of public discourse and its structuring conflicts. At one with the times in this at least, it is another kind of privatization.

A World Outside

Collini is at pains to defend the 'standing' and 'legitimacy' of his cultural criticism, as if believing that there would be plausibility or point in attacking it on those terms. He insists that this intellectual practice is none the worse for not being 'politics', leaving at least one reader to wonder who has been maintaining the contrary position. No, the simple question is how far it reaches *as criticism*, and how consequentially. The answer as I see it is, not very. The record of English cultural liberalism, to which Collini affiliates his work, has been variable in this decisive respect. Leavis based his assessments of the contemporary situation on a strong theory of historical modernity, from which he also derived the strategy and tactics of a cultural politics. That the theory was false and the politics desperate—and, increasingly, reactionary—is not the whole point: his critical practice was decided, biting, and, for many, an inspiration. Hoggart reinscribed a variety of that practice in the strategic narrative of the British labour movement, as an oblique reflection on its want of cultural percipience and ambition, its vulnerability to the intensifying commodification of popular life. His critical perspective guided a lifetime's work in cultural policy and administration. Collini seems closer to Hoggart than to any other figure in his twentieth-century tradition, while leaving far less tangible evidence of specific commitments or aspirations.[22] Having limited patience with

---

22   See his discussion of Hoggart in *English Pasts*, pp. 219–30.

theories and little taste for partisan division, he depends on his own resources, in a practice of criticism that is in all senses personal, and even private. In doing so, he defines a quietist variation in the movement of metacultural discourse, whose forms he retraces in all but the most important respect. Making no presumptuous metapolitical claims on public discourse, and harbouring no illusion that it already represents something better than it appears to, he slips through it as through something insubstantial, something not really there.

6

STEFAN COLLINI

On Variousness; and on Persuasion

As this is, I understand, to be the final instalment of the current exchange between Francis Mulhern and myself in these pages, it may be helpful if I try, very briefly, to summarize the main steps in the argument so far. I do not pretend this is an adequate account of the exchange in its entirety; it concentrates on what seems to me to have been the main locus of dispute between us, at least before the appearance of his most recent contribution.

The central argument of *Culture/Metaculture* may again be given in Mulhern's own words:

> 'Metaculture' names a modern discursive formation in which 'culture', however understood, speaks of its own generality and historical conditions of existence. Its inherent strategic impulse—failing which it would be no more than descriptive anthropology—is to mobilize 'culture' as a principle against the prevailing generality of 'politics' in the disputed plane of social authority. What speaks in metacultural discourse is the cultural principle itself, as it strives to dissolve the political as locus of general arbitration in social relations. Kulturkritik and Cultural Studies, typically contrasting in social attachment yet sharing this discursive template, have been strong versions of this metacultural will to authority.[1]

---

1 'Beyond Metaculture', above, p. 46.

On this view, what has been conventionally understood as 'cultural criticism'—which Mulhern, with polemical intent, redesignates as 'Kulturkritik'—stands accused of attempting to 'mediate a symbolic metapolitical resolution of the contradictions of capitalist modernity'. Only something properly describable as 'politics' rather than any form of 'metapolitics' could achieve a real resolution of these contradictions. Metacultural discourse is an attempt to 'supplant the authority of politics'; it 'dissolves the political'.[2] The nub of his argument is condensed in this one phrase.

My first response, while warmly appreciative of the book's merits, raised objections on two fronts, historical and conceptual. I objected that Mulhern's tightly defined category of 'Kulturkritik' could not, without distortion, embrace the wide range of intellectual figures to whom he wished to apply it. And I argued that Mulhern's own book, including its exhortation to practise a form of 'cultural politics', was itself a continuation of metacultural discourse, not a supersession of it; but that this was, in my view, no bad thing since to write from the perspective of culture does not, as Mulhern would have it, require an appeal to transcendentals: 'It only requires the presumption that disciplined reflection partly grounded in an extensive intellectual and aesthetic inheritance can furnish a place to stand in attempting to engage critically with the narrow pragmatism (or "specialism") of any particular political programme.'[3]

In his reply, 'Beyond Metaculture', Mulhern clarified and in some respects extended the argument of his book, particularly in relation to his category of 'Kulturkritik' and to the contrast he wishes to draw between the pernicious logic of all metacultural discourse and the legitimate enterprise of 'cultural politics'. He repeated that culture-as-principle asserts a 'claim to authority over the social whole' and thus that the attempt to displace politics was the 'inherent strategic impulse' of metacultural discourse. He characterized the role I had briefly sketched for cultural criticism

---

2 Mulhern, *Culture/Metaculture*, pp. 169, 166, and 'Culture/Metaculture', above, pp. 25, 13, 33, 22.

3 'Culture Talk', above, p. 40.

as governed by the logic of 'the Arnoldian problematic' and hence vitiated by the incoherence present in all metacultural discourse. He further extended the reach of his category of 'Kulturkritik' by proposing that a Marxist version of it was to be found in the work of Adorno and Marcuse. He reaffirmed the contrast with 'politics' understood as the reshaping of social patterns 'according to judgements based on a socially determinate programme and strategy'.[4] (It should be said that since I had not taken issue with the discussion of Cultural Studies in Mulhern's book, that aspect of the argument, which may be thought its most interesting and original element, has rather fallen from view in our subsequent exchange.)

In 'Defending Cultural Criticism', I acknowledged the ways in which Mulhern had clarified and extended his case, but I found this later version more troubling than the original. In an attempt to isolate the issues at stake, I essayed this brief summary of our areas of agreement:

> By this point, readers could be forgiven for feeling some frustration that Mulhern and I appear to agree on so much yet to differ on everything. We both insist on the non-identity of culture and politics; we both recognize politics as the important, inescapable, and difficult attempt to determine relations of power in a given space. We both have reservations about the extent to which so many on the left, especially the academic left, now treat questions of cultural identity, variously conceived, as the defining issues of politics. We both believe that those forms of criticism that seek to resolve the problems they diagnose simply by asserting the desirability or inevitability of some kind of harmony are indeed guilty of an evasion of politics. And we both seem drawn to a similar tone or writerly stance in discussing these matters, including a taste for certain kinds of intellectual irony. So, is there, in the end, any real difference between what he chooses to term 'cultural politics' and what I prefer to persist in calling 'cultural criticism'?

---

4   'Beyond Metaculture', above, pp. 61, 45–6, 65.

I elaborated on my objections to his now enlarged category of 'Kulturkritik' (on which more in a moment), and I asked whether for Mulhern there could be any 'cultural critics' who did *not* display the disabling failings of 'Kulturkritik', since it seems that for him public discourse belongs rightfully, and *exclusively*, to politics, while culture is always an intruder into this domain. I restated the familiar sense of 'cultural criticism', noting that in so doing I did 'not take myself to be saying anything particularly novel or to be staking out a distinctively personal position'. I again challenged the understanding of culture, influentially propounded by Raymond Williams, which sees it essentially as a compensatory projection of values excluded by the progress of 'capitalist modernity'. I urged that we do not have to understand culture in these functionalist, compensatory terms; that we should not attempt to make too clean or complete a division between 'culture' and 'society'; and that we do not need to regard *all* criticism of instrumental activity as presupposing or appealing to some 'transcendental realm'. I also urged that Mulhern's assertions *about* politics remain what he elsewhere calls 'metapolitics', indeed that what they offer might be described, applying his own phrase, as 'a symbolic metapolitical resolution of the contradictions of capitalist modernity'. I concluded that 'speaking about broadly political matters from a broadly cultural perspective is both legitimate and likely to be of limited effect. It is only one among the valuable forms of public debate, and by no means always the most important one.'[5]

I. What Is Cultural Criticism?

In his most recent contribution, 'What Is Cultural Criticism?',[6] Mulhern attempts to move the exchange into new territory. In particular, he engages with some of my writing from the past

---

5   'Defending Cultural Criticism', above, pp. 80, 68, 92, 86–7, 95.
6   Reprinted as Chapter 5, above, under the title 'The Logic of Cultural Criticism'.

fifteen years or so on the assumption that it represents the intellectual practice whose legitimacy I have thus far been attempting
to vindicate under the label of 'cultural criticism'. He detects in
that writing a certain vacancy, an absence of 'specific commitments', a lack of 'substantive critical value'. Along the way, he
generously identifies several positive qualities in my work, but in
the end it, too, is assigned to his overarching category of 'metacultural discourse', though it lacks the 'metapolitical' ambition hitherto constitutive of that discourse, and as a result merely offers a
'quietist variation' of it. In my own practice, therefore, I am held
to have exhibited the inadequacies that are inseparable from any
appeal to 'culture' in the criticism of society.[7]

It will be no great surprise that I wish to take issue with this
analysis at several points, but before dealing with what Mulhern
does say in his latest response, it is worth remarking what he does
not. First, he says nothing more about his construction of the
historical category of 'Kulturkritik' and my criticisms of it: he is
content, he declares, to let others 'weigh the arguments for themselves'. This seems intended to suggest a quiet confidence about
the persuasiveness of his own arguments, as well, perhaps, as a
weathered realism about the likely barrenness of further dispute.
But in fact Mulhern cannot stand pat at this point, since my objections, if not answered, are fatal for the viability of his larger
argument.

Under this head I had pressed two different types of objection.
The first was that this category is formulated at such a high level
of abstraction, and at such a great remove from the idioms and
concerns of those it is intended to embrace, that its use risks
distorting rather than illuminating. A strikingly wide variety of
figures—from Burke and Cobbett and Herder right through to
Mann and Benda and Ortega, and on to Adorno and Marcuse and
Orwell and Hoggart—are said to have 'acted within a shared
discursive order and subserved its governing logic'. But this
'discursive order' is not one that members of this alleged 'tradition' recognized themselves as sharing, and the alleged 'governing

---

7   Ibid., above, pp. 113, 106. 114.

logic', while discernible in a few cases, appears marginal or non-existent in others. The definition of the category is drawn too tightly: something that could be suggestive if presented as a series of family resemblances becomes obstructively Procrustean when made subject to one governing logic. The upshot is to weaken rather than strengthen the persuasiveness of 'Kulturkritik' as a (re)organizing idea.

My second objection was that although Mulhern claimed to define this category in formal terms, he in fact made certain historically specific elements constitutive of it. In commenting on the novel use made of the category of 'Kulturkritik' in *Culture/Metaculture*, I wrote that 'Mulhern makes European inter-war cultural pessimism its defining moment, so that the appeal to "culture" has to be socially elitist, culturally alarmist, and politically conservative'.[8] In his first reply, Mulhern denied this description, reiterating that the category was defined in formal terms and had no determinate political bearing. But as I suggested in return, the terms that he uses to characterize the thought of figures whom he discusses—'authoritarian', 'aristocratic', 'regressive'—surely indicate 'attitudes that most readers would recognize as broadly conservative in character'. Whatever positions the writers in question actually took in the politics of their time, assigning them to the tightly defined category of 'Kulturkritik' damns them for deploying a perspective that was 'authoritarian in final effect'. Moreover, some of the supposedly 'formal' properties in question are actually substantive and historical: for example, one of the defining tropes Mulhern proffers is 'modernity as disintegration', where the culminating feature of modernity turns out to be 'the rise of the masses'. The fact that this body of work was much given to identifying 'climacterics' and issuing a 'general alert' certainly seems to point towards my description of it as 'alarmist'. And, from another angle, the fact that a figure such as Croce may be described as having 'some formal affinity with Kulturkritik but perhaps no more substantial association' suggests that the

---

8   'Culture Talk', above, p. 36.

category is not wholly defined in formal terms.[9] In other words, Mulhern's transhistorical category of 'Kulturkritik' appears to be a generalization of features particularly to be found in the work of critics of 'mass society' in the inter-war period, but only selectively or faintly present in those writing in other periods or with other concerns. No one would dispute that several of these features are to be found in the cultural criticism of such figures as Thomas Mann or F. R. Leavis, to whom Mulhern returns with what I find to be a revealing frequency, but his deployment of the category allows him to tar all previous and subsequent cultural critics (now including me, it seems) with the same brush.

The unsustainable imperialism of his proposed new category can be indicated in a further way. *Culture/Metaculture*, the book in which Mulhern announces his category and sets it to work in reorganizing our understanding of twentieth-century intellectual history, draws on, and in places largely reprints, material from earlier essays. This is a common and unexceptionable practice (I am in no position to disapprove), but what is revealing in this case is that several passages have been reproduced more or less verbatim except that 'Kulturkritik' has now been silently substituted for a variety of interestingly different earlier terms. For example, in the later book he accounts for the lack of proper recognition of 'working-class self-organization in politics' in Hoggart's *The Uses of Literacy* in terms of 'the spontaneous perceptual effect of the convention that framed his analysis: that of Kulturkritik'. The same wording occurs in the earlier essay, save only that there the culprit is named as 'cultural criticism'. Or again, the later book speaks of Williams establishing 'the irreducible distance between Kulturkritik in all its variants—reactionary or reforming—and an integrally socialist politics of culture'. The same phrase occurs in the earlier essay, except that 'cultural liberalism' takes the place of 'Kulturkritik'. Or, finally, when Mulhern allows himself to register a rare note of reservation about Williams's work, he says of *Culture and Society* that its title concepts 'seemed often to exert reflexive control over his own discourse, deflecting

---

9 'Defending Cultural Criticism', above, p. 74.

his analytic and evaluative priorities away from political reason proper towards a "higher", finally "common" moral ground—the familiar orientation of Kulturkritik'. The phrasing in the original essay again displayed a revealing difference: 'reflexive control over his own discourse, inflecting his analytic and evaluative priorities towards a typically "humanist" derogation of political reason, with correlative intimations of a finally "common" moral interest'.[10] 'Cultural criticism', 'cultural liberalism', 'humanism'— whatever these disputed terms are taken to mean, they are far from identical. 'Kulturkritik', in Mulhern's new usage, elides distinctions in the present as well as the past in order to underwrite a polemical claim about 'political reason': this is surely the chief argument that readers will have to weigh for themselves.

The Elimination of Cultural Criticism

This leads on to the second and larger matter that Mulhern does not address in his latest response. He begins by asking 'what is the substance of the position' I wish to defend, and proffers an answer by means of 'an outline of [my] cultural criticism' as expressed in some of my more recent writing. I shall return in a moment to the hasty assumption that the position I have been defending thus far in this exchange must be represented by my own practice—indeed, that the defence of that practice is the unavowed impulse behind my general argument. But what is most striking about this tactic is that it makes no acknowledgement of the fact that the polemical thrust of Mulhern's initial position, as set out in *Culture/Metaculture* and defended in his subsequent essay, was to deny the possibility of any legitimate form of cultural criticism and to propose to replace it with his own version of 'cultural politics'.

---

10   Mulhern, *Culture/Metaculture*, pp. 59, 72, 67; cf. *The Present Lasts a Long Time*, pp. 122, 130, 127. The next sentence after this last passage speaks of *Culture and Society* as Williams's 'revaluation of English Kulturkritik' where the original had spoken of 'revaluation of English cultural criticism', and so on. As I noted in 'Culture Talk', above, p. 33, the relevant essay, 'A Welfare Culture? Hoggart and Williams in the Fifties', appeared first in *Radical Philosophy* in 1996 and was then reprinted in *Present* before being extensively re-used in *Culture/Metaculture*.

My earlier contributions did indeed involve a 'defence' of the possibility of a legitimate form of cultural criticism, but precisely because a defence seemed called for in the face of his attack. Again I offered a series of arguments against the sweepingness of his initial claims, but again his most recent contribution does not attempt to respond to these objections. It is important, therefore, to restate the nub of this disagreement before we can proceed to judge whether the remarks he makes about some of my other writings are to the point.

As we have just seen, Mulhern has for some time been training his sights on what he called the 'typically "humanist" derogation of political reason'. Here, the scare-quotes are the typographical expression of the curled lip, set against the almost Kantian grandeur bestowed by speaking of 'political reason' rather than simply 'politics'. Expanding the range of targets in his recent book, he attacked what he described as 'the utopian impulse, common to the old cultural criticism and the new cultural studies, to resolve the tension of the relationship between culture and politics by dissolving political reason itself'.[11] In response, I disputed this claim, not least because it seemed to propose a restrictive and tendentious understanding of 'the old cultural criticism'. I restated a fairly conventional understanding of that activity (hence my insistence that the position I was occupying was neither novel nor distinctively personal), an activity in which the intellectual and aesthetic practices loosely denominated as 'culture' provide a series of resources or perspectives from which to engage in the criticism of society, including its largely instrumental activities, as well as criticism of the work of other critics. Mulhern has still not established that this must, in principle, be an illegitimate activity.

I had said that this was the sense 'associated, in Britain, with aspects of the work of figures such as Matthew Arnold, T. S. Eliot, George Orwell, Richard Hoggart, and so on'.[12] In his most recent piece, Mulhern immediately begins by summarizing my account

---

11 Mulhern, *Culture/Metaculture*, pp. xx–xxi, and 'Culture/Metaculture', above, pp. 10–11.
12 'Defending Cultural Criticism', above, p. 68.

and then saying, having quoted this illustrative list: 'This is recognizable as a self-description (except in its evocation of Eliot, whom I for one would not have thought to associate with Collini's critical journalism).'[13] What strikes me here is not the assumption that I have all along been offering a covert defence of my own critical practice, but the suggestion that Eliot's name is somehow out of place in the list, that he is too unlike the others mentioned—perhaps on account of his provokingly reactionary views? This is the first place (more are to come) where I sense that Mulhern naturally tends to assume that an activity or tradition presupposes substantive agreement. If I *had* been offering, with extreme presumption, a sly self-description in the passage in question, I would not have found Eliot's inclusion incongruous, however much I might recoil from some of his unappealing political stances and social attitudes. The truth surely is that anyone drawing up a short shortlist of names illustrative of the genre of cultural criticism in twentieth-century Britain would be likely to include Eliot, without thereby identifying with or endorsing his (or any of the other names') practice of the activity.

A similar problem surfaces when Mulhern, in the course of disputing the coherence of the sense of 'cultural criticism' I have invoked, juxtaposes T. S. Eliot, Raymond Williams and Richard Hoggart as 'three reflective, critically distant contributions to post-war discussion of culture and society', and then concludes, with the air of a prosecuting counsel who has just clinched his case: 'They all meet Collini's minimum criteria for cultural criticism, and they are mutually incompatible.'[14] Well, if 'incompatible' means they exhibit or champion different intellectual styles and political values, then they are indeed 'incompatible', but that doesn't make them any the less practitioners of forms of cultural criticism. To say that the formal characteristics I had mentioned, such as distance, reflectiveness, and generality, do not enable us to 'set about discriminating among' these three writers is not an objection to characterizing cultural criticism partly in these

---

13 'The Logic of Cultural Criticism', above, p. 98.
14 Ibid., p. 101.

general terms. Of course there would be other features and other values in terms of which one could discriminate among them; the three characteristics mentioned could never be supposed to be all that one would bring to reading them. In almost any field, writers and thinkers can be classified as engaged in a common activity while holding wildly divergent views about aspects of its subject-matter. There is no damaging case to be answered here.

Culture, Again

I have to confess that I am not sure if there is a case to be answered with respect to Mulhern's paragraphs on the different senses of 'culture'. I am owning up to a genuine difficulty of understanding here, not essaying a lofty put-down, but the paragraphs in question are highly condensed and not easy to interpret. I take Mulhern to be saying that even the conventional sense of 'culture' which I invoked is now so shot through with theoretical contention as to render incoherent any idea of the critic appealing to and speaking from its perspectives and values. Either it tacitly lays claim to an unsustainable superiority over the world of non-culture, requiring some version of Arnold's 'best self' to validate the position from which it speaks, or else, rethought as an aspect of 'the relations between elements in a whole way of life', it loses any independent standing vis-à-vis 'the divided historical world of sense'. I repudiated the former position, without, allegedly, properly appreciating how the latter understanding undercuts the possibility of criticism being furnished by 'culture' with an enabling perspective or set of resources, since art and ideas themselves, thus understood, will tend to operate 'within the space of the ideological dominant'. To support this, he cites Williams's analysis, in *Culture and Society*, of the mid-nineteenth-century industrial novel 'in which strong, eloquent witness to the reality of working-class suffering coexisted, imaginatively, with an ungovernable fear of mass irrationality', and he goes on to argue that even when literature takes culture itself as its material, it is still subject to 'such disturbance of vision'.[15]

---

15   Ibid., above, pp. 99–100.

As can sometimes happen with briskly handled historical instances, the chosen example here appears rather to call the main argument into- question than to support it. To speak of these novels suffering from 'disturbance of vision' implies possession of the clear or undisturbed vision that they might have manifested had it not been for the pressure exerted by 'the ideological dominant'. But does that correct, undisturbed vision thus escape 'the divided historical world of sense'? If it does, then the general form of the objection seems null: if Engels can have access to such vision then so, in principle, can Mrs Gaskell. But if it doesn't so escape, then the general objection is null for the opposite reason: being part of 'the divided historical world of sense' does not necessarily prevent writers from arriving at a penetratingly critical grasp of aspects of the society in which they live. This latter proposition seems to me broadly true and borne out by frequent historical example (which is one reason why the notion of 'the ideological dominant' always threatens to overreach itself). But in that case, the practitioners of 'cultural criticism' and 'cultural politics' are in exactly the same boat: neither group has, nor needs, access to some privileged source of 'undisturbed' vision; both manage to fashion criticisms of contemporary society out of the materials to hand.

In discussing Mulhern's example I have left aside the question of whether one should expect a *novel* to offer a single, unambiguous, analysis of a given social issue; perhaps the 'imaginative coexistence' of different planes or registers of experience is part of what we find distinctive and distinctively valuable about fiction. But the fact that, in offering his example, Mulhern himself does not seem at all troubled by this thought suggests to me a possible interpretation of his more abstract—and, to my eye, somewhat more opaque—general statements about 'culture'.

In talking about the extended, more anthropological, notion of 'culture' favoured in the later work of Williams and the style of cultural studies claiming descent from it, Mulhern observes that literature and philosophy persist as part of 'the social relations of meaning as a whole', and then he adds: 'Were it not so, the new concept of culture would simply invert the dualism of the old.'

But what is this 'dualism' and in what sense does the allegedly new concept of culture not share in it, whatever it is? Here is where I feel most uncertain in my reading of Mulhern, but the charge of dualism (it is clearly intended as a charge) seems to rest on the assumption that the cultural critic takes literature and ideas to be somehow apart from or above society, and hence reifies culture as—in the term with which Williams critically summarized the outcome of the history he surveyed—'an abstraction and an absolute'. I would remark in passing that it is not obvious to me that all the figures whom Williams discussed did reify culture in this way, but in any event there is no reason whatever to assume that the contemporary cultural critic *must* do so. Of course cultural activities are 'part of society'; all human activities are 'part of society' (what else could they be part of?), including the activity of 'seeking to determine the shape of social relations as a whole in a given space'. To speak of 'culture' as, for certain purposes, distinguishable from 'society' is no more to be the prisoner of a disabling 'dualism' than it is to speak of 'politics' as, for certain purposes, distinguishable from 'society'. In the course of their writing, any writer establishes, both propositionally and symptomatically, how alert they are to the element of arbitrary convention involved in such categories. But, handled with the requisite self-consciousness, 'culture' is as useful and legitimate a term in this context as is 'politics'.

Following the sequence of Mulhern's most recent response, a very brief exegetical digression is required here. I had remarked that in much of the literature on this topic, as in this exchange itself, 'politics' tended to be used with two different emphases. There was what I called 'the conventional, newspaper reader's sense—the everyday doings of politicians, parties, and parliaments'; and there was the 'more elevated' sense, 'the attempt to order social relations in the light of conceptions of human possibility'.[16] Mulhern's invocation of 'political reason itself' clearly shares this second emphasis; the disparaging remarks by some cultural critics about 'the routine reproduction of

---

16   'Defending Cultural Criticism', above, p. 83.

controversies or competitive interests' just as clearly partake of the
first (Raymond Williams helpfully provides the illustrative phrase
in this case). Mulhern berates me for appealing to 'the authority'
of the newspaper reader, and then proceeds to read me a long,
unnecessary sermon on the way large issues about contrasting
visions of human society suffuse everyday newspaper reports,
something especially visible at times of heightened conflict, such
as Weimar Germany or, in a different way, Thatcher's Britain.
Indeed so: it is hard to imagine anyone ever wanting to deny that.
But it was surely clear that I was not *appealing* to 'the authority'
of the newspaper reader, whatever that would be; I was simply
using a familiar piece of shorthand. I was not trying to introduce
some new piece of conceptual machinery here, merely remarking
a movement between emphases, a movement which has been
remarked before but which, if not attended to, fosters confusion
about the level of discourse or activity in question. A critic may
reasonably call attention to instances of short-termism, careerism,
and cynicism in aspects of contemporary political life without
thereby being guilty of attempting 'to dissolve political reason
itself'.

Varieties of Criticism

In my earlier contribution, I observed that the question at issue is
obviously closely bound up with ways of understanding the role
of 'the intellectual'. In response, Mulhern offers us two alternatives. There is the 'corporatist' conception: 'intellectuals are in
principle a cohesive social group, bonded morally in a commitment to universals by virtue of which they pass judgement on the
world'. Set over against this is a more modest conception which
recognizes that 'the characteristic practice of intellectuals is one
modality of intervention among others in the contested field of
social relations'; 'intellectuals make their choices from a range of
historical possibilities that they share with everyone'. He correctly
surmises that the first of these alternatives is 'not an option' for
me, but he also suspects that the second accords the intellectual
even less 'status' than I would wish to do, since (I extrapolate from

his other remarks) it reserves no distinctive content for 'culture' in the name of which I see the intellectual as speaking.[17]

I have to begin by saying that I would not choose to work within this binary pairing, but I do not, in fact, want to reserve any special status for intellectuals. That term has come to be principally applied to those who, from a basis in some creative, scholarly, or other cultural achievement, address a non-specialist audience on matters of general concern. That is, in Mulhern's terms, their distinctive 'modality of intervention', but it is distinctive enough for the purpose and is different from 'intervening' on the basis of, say, one's commercial or legal role. But while this may still seem to Mulhern to be claiming too much for the activity of intellectuals, it also seems to him to be claiming too little. 'If intellectual practice is really so modestly specified, after all, what position can it sustain?'[18] But what does 'position' refer to here? Intellectual practice is intellectual practice, modestly specified or not (and if there is to be a choice, then a little modesty in such matters seems more appealing than its opposite). There's no great mystery about it, nor about the ways in which one might draw upon its protocols in criticizing contemporary society. What 'position' *may* mean, as indicated by Mulhern's reference in the previous paragraph to the 'social grounding' of 'universals', is a set of views which endorse or promote the interests of a particular social class. But to ask for 'universals' would already be one contestable move; to assume they only have any validity when 'socially grounded' in this way would be another (and saying this is not to be committed to 'Idealism'). It is part of my overall case that one does not *have* to speak in these terms.

It is, presumably, largely for this reason that Mulhern claims to detect a kind of vacancy or absence at the heart of my writing in this area. 'This reduced idea of the intellectual, like the abstract "perspective of culture" with which [Collini] now very plausibly associates it, is a piece of algebra: y to the other's x, it is a cipher

---

17 'The Logic of Cultural Criticism', above, p. 106.
18 Ibid.

awaiting its substantive critical value.'[19] Clearly, something about my writing frustrates and irritates Mulhern, but this expression of his frustration does not advance the argument. Any 'idea of the intellectual' will be principally a characterization of a relation—a relation between a public, a medium, an occasion, a reputation and so on. It can obviously not be specified in terms of expressing only one kind of view, nor is a commentator, in analysing 'the idea of the intellectual', thereby endorsing one kind of view over others.

Mulhern is sufficiently pleased with the conceit of 'algebra' to repeat it, as when he lists several things which I, as an intellectual historian, am interested in, such as manner, tone, temper and so on, and comments: 'So the algebraic series continues.'[20] But are such matters really such an empty notational code, a deferral of 'substance'? Differences of temper, for example, are not just among the most interesting differences distinguishing human beings from each other; they may be highly consequential as well, and to attend to those differences is not necessarily to withdraw one's attention from a public to a private sphere. The 'substance', against which such empty algebra is contrasted, seems to be provided by differences of 'political evaluation', the deliverances of 'political reason itself'. But these are the phrases which seem vulnerable, if any are, to the charges of 'vacancy' and the deferral of substance. Here we seem to be in that topsy-turvy world in which proclaiming one's general allegiance to some supposed direction of world history counts as 'substantive', whereas offering some individual characterization or detailed critical discrimination is derogated as mere 'algebra'. And this returns us to the question of why '*political* evaluation' should automatically be thought to trump all other kinds: sometimes it quite properly does and sometimes, surely, it does not.

---

19   Ibid.
20   Ibid., p. 108.

II. Doing Cultural Criticism

The greater part of Mulhern's most recent essay is given over to an extended critique of some of my writing during the past couple of decades. I should say immediately that, flattering though this critique is in some ways, it strikes me as largely irrelevant to the matter in hand. In trying to reinstate the possibility of some legitimate form of cultural criticism, in the face of its elimination in Mulhern's conceptual scheme, I did not intend to be justifying any practice of my own. The case was made in general terms because it was a general possibility whose legitimacy had been called into question. However, since Mulhern has now proceeded in this way, and since he clearly believes that his critical observations on my writing do serve to discredit the case for cultural criticism more generally, I shall try to respond to his criticisms, aware of the perils of self-justification and the kinds of intellectual egotism to which it can lead.

I should begin by declaring that I do not think of myself as having been a 'cultural critic' with a consistent and distinctive practice, not least because very little of what I have written until quite recently would have any claim to be regarded as 'cultural criticism' in the first place. For many years all of my work, and even now the larger part of it, has been recognizable as a contribution to intellectual history, pursued in a scholarly and (as it has seemed to some readers) rather austere mode. For several years, now, it is true, I have also written occasional pieces that attempt to address a wider, non-specialist readership, though I am not sure whether these pieces, most of which have taken the form of review-essays, count as even minor contributions to the activity of 'cultural criticism' as that term has conventionally been understood. More generally, my intellectual development has been slow and uneven, making me less confident and less settled about the direction of my thinking than Mulhern himself seems to have been from a comparatively early stage. One or two of the cited examples of my work, especially from some time ago, all too visibly bear the marks of someone trying to find his way.

In the late 1970s and 1980s, in addressing aspects of nineteenth-century British intellectual history that also figured as part of the subject-matter of the sub-fields of the history of the social sciences and the history of political thought, I was particularly concerned to try to rescue the quiddity of past historical agents from the schematizing and present-minded treatment they often received from social scientists and political theorists raiding the past to support some contemporary theoretical position. I have since come to see that *Public Moralists* (completed in 1990 and drawing on material from the previous decade) would have been a better book if I had not allowed a desire to escape from under the shadow of the 'history of political theory' to shape my mode of address in places, and Mulhern is justified in detecting an irritable insistence in some of my more sweeping remarks from that period about the coerciveness of 'doctrines' and 'theories'.

Nonetheless, even in my own case I acknowledge the truth of Dr Johnson's observation that 'he who writes much will not easily escape a manner, such a recurrence of particular modes as may be easily noted',[21] and I recognize some of the continuities in manner and mode to which Mulhern draws attention. But the larger case, which he prosecutes with no little forensic zeal, simply does not stand up. Mulhern is, needless to say, under no obligation to give a comprehensive and proportioned account of my work, but since he furnishes several summary characterizations of it and then uses those characterizations to criticize or discredit the activity of cultural criticism more generally, it seems necessary to point out at least some of the ways in which his reading of me risks being tendentious or culpably selective.

Back to Arnold?

Mulhern makes much of my handling of particular figures, such as Matthew Arnold, Richard Hoggart and Christopher Hitchens, so let me take each case in turn. The chief reservation I have about

21   Samuel Johnson, 'The Life of Dryden', in *Lives of the Poets*, (1779–81), quoted in Christopher Ricks, *Allusion to the Poets*, Oxford 2002, p. 42.

his discussion of my writing on Matthew Arnold, a reservation I should like to think any reader of that writing would share, is that it rests on a too-ready identification of author and subject. It is clearly the case that there are aspects of Arnold's writing that I find winning, and in the Preface to my brief 'Past Masters' volume I explained why, writing on that subject at that moment in that format, I had chosen to present a portrait that some might consider 'culpably indulgent'. But sympathetic recreation does not entail endorsement. Indeed, in the concluding chapter I made clear that I am not one of Arnold's 'most devoted champions', and I hoped the book had indicated some of the ways in which I thought him 'most liable to criticism'.[22] Mulhern nonetheless persists in reading me as 'not far apart' from Arnold on various crucial matters, concluding from one passage in my exposition that, 'if the free indirect style allows a confident reading', I am not speaking 'at any significant distance' from the views I am describing.[23] I am surprised that anyone trained in literary criticism, as Mulhern was, should so confidently identify me with views reported through this particular literary strategy. This general case is then buttressed by what seem to me misreadings of particular passages. For example, he cites my speaking of Arnold's 'deep intellectual affinity' with Platonism which I took as one indication of 'what might be described as the "anti-political" character of his thought'. Mulhern reads this as straightforward endorsement on my part, though I would have thought the original text was sufficiently clear on the matter. In the paragraph from which Mulhern quotes, I say: 'Arnold was temperamentally something of a Platonist, with all the Platonist's vulnerability to being dazzled by the beauty of his own ideals to the neglect of their abuse in practice.' I go on to say in the immediately succeeding paragraph: 'No one with such a strong aversion to conflict as Arnold came to manifest could be an altogether satisfactory writer on politics.'[24] I cannot see how these sentences could be

---

22 Collini, *Arnold*, pp. vii, 117.
23 'The Logic of Cultural Criticism', above, p. 104.
24 Collini, *Arnold*, pp. 91–2.

read as other than criticisms, criticisms which emphasize the limitations of 'the "anti-political" character of his thought' and which surely signal a more than temporal distance separating historical author and modern commentator.

Since Mulhern has already paid me the compliment of reading several things that I have written, it may seem ungracious on my part to reproach him with not reading more, but given that he makes so much of my supposed identification with Arnold's views, I think he should feel obliged to take into account the explicit reflections on this question that appear in the Afterword to the Clarendon Press re-issue of the 'Past Masters' volume.[25] Although I there acknowledged that in the first edition I may have been naïve in not anticipating how reductively my sympathetic portrait of Arnold could be construed, I reiterated, in pretty plain terms, my sense of distance from not just his 'severest detractors' but his 'zealous champions' as well: 'I have no wish to defend all of Arnold's particular judgements or tastes . . . Similarly, the notion of trying to "imitate" Arnold's performance seems to me fundamentally misguided, only capable, even at its best, of yielding wilful anachronism and mannered pastiche.' And I singled out for criticism those modern readers who do attempt to endorse Arnold in the way Mulhern objects to: 'I have no sympathy with the . . . appropriation of this particular Victorian writer to add a historical veneer to an intransigent anti-modernism.'[26]

Mulhern himself, of course, is not prey to any incriminating sympathy or even ambivalence on the subject: 'Bourgeois society defined Arnold's imaginative horizon.' He immediately moves to what he takes to be the telling contrast: 'Marx saw in the same society the conditions of a qualitatively superior collective life beyond it, to be achieved by political means.' Mulhern is confident in these ascriptions; he is confident that they are the only real choices; and he is confident that this divide is what matters above all others. He and I must accordingly be slotted into this template;

25 Afterword in Collini, *Matthew Arnold*, pp. 125–38.
26 Ibid., pp. 134, 137, 131–2.

he knows where he stands, and now he feels reasonably confident he has put me in my box, too.

The niceties of my relation to the work of Matthew Arnold (or of any other historical figure) are not, I suspect, of very wide interest, but it seemed important to pause on this example because it exhibits a recurring feature of Mulhern's case. I sense in his most recent essay an insistent urge to classify and label me. As in his previous contribution, one of the ways he attempts to do this is by establishing what he takes to be my preferred historical affiliations, but he consistently over-reads these and finds political endorsement where there is only imaginative sympathy. This accounts for his disproportionately frequent return to my supposed alignment of myself with Richard Hoggart. One reason this seems to me disproportionate (in a way that his case about Arnold, whatever its other defects, does not) is that I have only ever published half of one essay about Hoggart, a piece that began as a review of one of his later books, *Townscape with Figures*. I clearly found that an interesting book, and I used it to illustrate what I took to be certain admirable and attractive features in the personal ethos of Hoggart's writing more generally.[27] But I have never attempted any thorough discussion of his work or even given parts of it the kind of close analytical scrutiny I have devoted to, say, Eliot, Leavis, or Williams. The truth is that Hoggart figures much more substantially in *Mulhern's* work than in mine, and is for him an important negative reference point.[28] I suspect I may be partly to blame for his reading a little too much into my brief discussion, because in revising it for republication I made it one half of a diptych in which I contrasted Hoggart with Raymond Williams, especially in terms of their styles as *writers*, where the

---

27   Reprinted in Collini, *English Pasts*, pp. 219–30. I should say, in case any significance could be thought to attach to my not saying, that I subsequently met and got to know Hoggart a little, and also that he later wrote a measured but largely positive review of *English Pasts*.

28   See, for example, his essay 'A Welfare Culture?', reproduced in *The Present Lasts a Long Time*, and the sections of *Culture/Metaculture* entitled 'Hoggart and the Abuses of Literacy', 'Literature and Contemporary Cultural Studies', and 'From Hoggart to Stuart Hall'.

balance of judgement seems to me to favour Hoggart. This is obviously not all I would say about either of them from other points of view, especially Williams, but Mulhern reads it as a defining declaration of allegiance.

Huntin' with Hitchens?

The single piece of my writing which Mulhern subjects to the most extended scrutiny is a review-essay on Christopher Hitchens's *Orwell's Victory*, which appeared in the *London Review of Books* in 2003.[29] The burden of his objection here appears to be that I remain too close to my subject both stylistically and in cultural reference. Noting that the idea of 'company' crops up several times, especially in the piece's closing vignette, he finds me altogether too 'convivial', though after rereading my piece I have to say that Mulhern must have a more bracing and strenuous sense of 'conviviality' than I do. But the force of his objection rests, yet again, on what I do not do, or do not do sufficiently emphatically. Above all, he notes I only make one reference to 'Hitchens's support for Bush's wars of aggression' and that I do so in wording that is said to 'ease readers past the political crisis to which it alludes'. The phrase in question—about Hitchens's position on the invasion of Iraq putting him in 'some very unlovely company'— may itself be thought too oblique or even arch, but yet again I would have to say that an essayist has to be allowed some choice about his point of access to a topic and his mode of address. 'Hitchens's support for Bush's wars of aggression' is certainly one legitimate topic, but it is not the only one; in this case, it also happened to be one that several other writers had already written about. I see no reason to regard it as the key or the ultimate destination of all of Hitchens's writing, or as somehow more central than the features of that writing which I do discuss. Yet again, we seem to be back with the overriding status Mulhern ascribes to

29   Collini, ' "No Bullshit" Bullshit'; since Mulhern notes that 'Hitchens rather than Orwell is indeed the subject', I should perhaps record that this was at the request of the editors of the *LRB*.

political affiliation understood in elemental friend–foe terms. Commenting on the concluding paragraph of my piece, he complains that 'the burden of [my] judgement remains . . . not fully public in the expected way'.[30] It is not clear to me who is doing the expecting here, but my sense of the readers of the *LRB* is that they are a sophisticated and diverse lot, well able to appreciate the burden of judgement even of a piece liberally salted with 'high-spirited irony'.

Generalizing from this example to the limitations of my cultural criticism as a whole, Mulhern declares: 'This is criticism as home truths. Home truths have force but little scope.'[31] But surely the point about 'home truths' is that they have precisely the scope that is appropriate to the occasion: that is what makes them effective. Here, and not for the first time, I find myself wondering what kind of effectiveness Mulhern, were he to have been writing in that paper on that occasion, would feel was desirable and attainable. In any event, the kind of 'scope' he finds lacking in my criticism is suggested by his immediately passing, in the same paragraph, to the question of the possibility of the 'transformation' of 'the social relations of capitalism', and he in effect reproves me for not conducting my examination of Hitchens by the light of an explicit declaration of where I stand on this. But I trust I have by now made clear why I do not share his sense of the constant obligatoriness of that exercise.

Scarcely Political?

More generally, I hope I have also made clear that I do not accept the terms in which Mulhern no less constantly draws a contrast between 'real' or 'substantive commitments' and the matters of voice, tone, perspective and so on that much of my writing has focused on. The universal applicability and usefulness of a distinction framed in these terms is part of what is at issue between us. But even according to Mulhern's preferred conceptual vocabulary,

---

30 'The Logic of Cultural Criticism', above, p. 112.
31 Ibid.

it has to be said that he does not properly acknowledge, or give the reader an adequate sense of, the place that such 'substantive commitments' do have in my writing. My alleged failings in this respect are summed up in summary fashion indeed: 'The terms of evaluation that he brings to public discourse are scarcely political, even where politics is the matter in hand.'[32] It is, of course, possible that Mulhern is working with an esoteric and hard-to-measure-up-to sense of what is to count as 'political' here, but I fear that he may just be exaggerating a fair comment on some parts of my work into a false generalization about the whole of it.

For brevity's sake, let me confine my counterexamples to those available in the sources he himself makes use of, the kind of essay collected in *English Pasts* and the kind of essay recently published in the *London Review of Books*. Thus, writing in the former about the Tory Party's appeal to 'Victorian values' in the 1980s, I hardly hid my hostility to 'policies that manifestly make the rich richer and the poor poorer', or my support for those measures from earlier in the century that 'had, until the 1980s, made Britain a less horrible country to be poor in', or more generally my disdain for 'the gutter individualism of the 1980s and 1990s'.[33] Since Mulhern rests so much of his case on a piece from the *LRB* that was allegedly characteristic of my writing in avoiding 'political' terms of evaluation, perhaps I may quote at some length from a slightly earlier essay in those pages. Thus, when writing about the fantasy of 'England' promoted by Roger Scruton, whom I characterized as 'a born-again Tory ideologue masquerading as a once-born countryman', I spoke of his evasion of the fact that 'those who control great concentrations of wealth can systematically determine the life-chances of the many who do not', and went on: 'At such moments, all this sub-Waugh attitudinising ceases to seem amiably harmless, and falls into place as part of a wider cultural tendency whose effect is to distract our attention from

---

32   Ibid. I leave aside, as an uncharacteristically cheap shot that stands self-condemned, his jibe that my style of cultural criticism is 'at one with the times' in being 'another kind of privatization'.

33   Collini, *English Pasts*, pp. 106, 110, 114.

what "the experience of class" is actually about.' And at the end of the essay, I offered some more general thoughts that do not, on rereading, seem chiefly distinguished by their avoidance of political terms of evaluation:

> For the fact is that the unsleeping destructive energy of capital seeking to maximise its returns is not going to be tamed by a spot of huntin', shootin', and fishin'. It is not going to be tamed by a spot of Anglicanism, either, or any other prettied-up form of 're-enchantment'. It might, possibly, be tamed by a spot of Socialism.

I then concluded: 'And this, surely, is the disabling paradox of modern "conservatism", namely that it wants simultaneously to liberate market forces and to lament the effects of market forces. Hence the deep structural dilemma of the modern Tory social critic: the forces that are destroying all that he loves are the forces he is ideologically committed to supporting.'[34] I would have thought there was enough 'political evaluation' here to satisfy even Mulhern. But it is perfectly true that I don't think this is *always* what needs saying—and so on such occasions I don't say it.

It may also be to the point to mention a more recent piece anatomizing the assumptions informing current New Labour policy on universities—to the point because although it appeared too late for Mulhern to have taken it into account, its concerns and critical intent are continuous with those in a couple of pieces published in the 1980s on higher education policy which are included in *English Pasts*.[35] I trust the terms in which I analyse public discourse here could not be stigmatized as 'scarcely political'. Of course, Mulhern may, like any other reader, have objections to or reservations about the piece, but I hope it may serve as an example of one form of cultural criticism which engages with a pressing contemporary

---

34 Stefan Collini, 'Hegel in Green Wellies', *London Review of Books*, 8 January 2001 (reviewing Roger Scruton, *England: An Elegy*, London 2000, and Kenneth Baker, ed., *The Faber Book of Landscape Poetry*, London 2000).

35 'HiEdBiz', *London Review of Books*, 6 November 2003.

issue without tending, even implicitly, to authoritarianism or nostalgia.

Mulhern concludes his assessment of my work with a most curious closing paragraph. He writes that I insist that my intellectual practice (which I had not actually been writing about) 'is none the worse for not being "politics", leaving at least one reader to wonder who has been maintaining the contrary position'.[36] This is disingenuous in the extreme: our whole exchange has pivoted around Mulhern's indictment of cultural criticism, as part of 'metacultural discourse', for its 'inherent' impulse to 'displace politics, dissolve political reason itself'. But this, he says, is not the issue where my 'intellectual practice' is concerned (though it is he who has concerned it): 'No, the simple question is how far it reaches *as criticism*, and how consequentially. The answer as I see it is not very.' Expressed in a more sympathetic spirit, this would be to raise a very interesting, if in some ways intractable, question about any criticism, mine (for what it is worth) included. How *do* we judge the reach and impact of criticism? 'Reach' here is presumably intellectual as well as social, with the implication that since my criticism doesn't reach much beyond matters of voice and temperament, it is hardly surprising that it is ineffective in changing society. Well, I certainly wouldn't want to make any large claims for the effectiveness of what I write, but I can't help wondering a bit about the presumed effectiveness of other modes. May it not be that offering a reasonably wide and heterogeneous range of readers some prompts to re-examining what they think they know has a claim to being as 'effective', in its own way, as advancing a set of theoretical claims, couched at a high level of abstraction, to a small and largely converted set of readers? I wouldn't myself want to give priority to any one measure of effectiveness or to dismiss any of these forms of criticism out of hand, but the comparison leaves me thinking that each form has its own distinctive limitations when it comes to reach and effectiveness.

But I, apparently, 'affiliate' my work to 'English cultural liberalism', a tradition whose record 'has been variable in this decisive

---

36   'The Logic of Cultural Criticism', above, p. 113.

respect'. The decisive respect, remember, is 'how far it reaches *as criticism*, and how consequentially'. In a revealing move, Mulhern suggests that in fact not all criticism in this manner has been as inconsequential as mine has. For example:

> Leavis based his assessments of the contemporary situation on a strong theory of historical modernity, from which he also derived the strategy and tactics of a cultural politics. That the theory was false and the politics desperate—and, increasingly, reactionary—is not the whole point: his critical practice was decided, biting, and, for many, an inspiration.[37]

The rhetorical emphasis here may seem to suggest that it is more important to *have* a 'theory' and to *have* a 'politics', even if they are false, desperate and reactionary, than it is to try to conduct one's 'assessments of the contemporary situation' (in so far as that is what one wishes to address, which it is not always) in more accurate and discriminating, but acknowledgedly piecemeal and incomplete, ways. Leavis's 'strong theory of historical modernity' was, as Mulhern knows better than anyone, an eclectic amalgam of nostalgia, prejudice and moral austerity, interspersed with some perceptive observations about the changing shapes of an 'educated reading public'. Neither Leavis's nor anyone else's assessments of the contemporary situation were made more probing or more analytical for being based on the historical fantasy of a lost 'organic community'. (It is incidentally interesting to see that, since he is being cited with some measure of approval on this occasion, Leavis is allowed to have practised a 'cultural politics', though normally he figures in Mulhern's indictment of the 'Kulturkritik' tradition as an exponent of 'cultural criticism'.) The passage also sheds an interesting light on Mulhern's recurrent engagement with Leavis during the past twenty-five years. It suggests he sees him as an opponent worth attending to, partly because one can respect the moral strenuousness of his hostility to 'technologico-Benthamite civilization', and partly because, by

---

37   Ibid.

attempting to develop a 'theory of historical modernity' and to derive a 'cultural politics' from it, Leavis could be regarded as making explicit what was merely presumed by more implicit or evasive forms of 'cultural liberalism'. Demolishing the 'false' theory and the 'desperate' politics is then not only invitingly easy, but it can also claim to be a telling and representative victory.

As it happens, I, too, have a long-standing interest in, and not a little respect for, Leavis, at least for his early literary criticism (rather less for his cultural criticism), and it is true that his particular combination of critical acuity and moral intensity attracted a considerable number of followers in certain circles in England, and elsewhere, in the middle decades of the twentieth century. But in an essay that there is no particular reason for Mulhern to have cited, or even to have been aware of, I have tried to indicate why Leavis seems to me to be more of a warning than an inspiration where criticism of society is concerned, not least on account of the absence in his work of 'any adequately sociological understanding of his own society, and a consequent inability to estimate social and political forces at their true strength'. As it also happens, I there offer further strictures on 'the tradition of literary critics as social critics that descended from Arnold' and itemize some of the 'common sins of cultural criticism carried out in this mode'.[38] It perhaps throws some light on differences of 'temper' between Mulhern and myself (if I may be allowed to take a favourite hobby-horse out for a short canter here) that he, despite fundamental reservations about the political logic of Leavis's work, emphasizes his regard for the reach of his cultural criticism on account of its 'theorized' and 'biting' character, whereas I, despite some regard for Leavis's work as a teacher and critic of literature, am more deterred by the superficiality and exaggeration characteristic of his cultural criticism.

More generally, Mulhern observes, quite justly, that one of my preferred forms is the intellectual portrait. However, he detects a

---

38   Stefan Collini, 'The Critic as Anti-journalist: Leavis after *Scrutiny*', in Jeremy Treglown and Bridget Bennett, eds, *Grub Street and the Ivory Tower: Literary Journalism and Literary Scholarship from Fielding to the Internet*, Oxford 1998, pp. 151–76, at p. 172.

sinister theoretical significance in this preference. For the 'unargued premise' of my work turns out to be 'one of the central commonplaces of literary-liberal culture in the twentieth century', namely that 'literature . . . is to public discourse what the individual person is to the social order, the limit of classifying presumption'.[39] On another occasion one might pause to ask what authorizes this coarsely aggregative use of 'liberal'; similarly, 'commonplace' suggests that we are dealing with something that is taken to be mere common sense by members of that 'culture', but which can be seen for the peculiar or ideological belief it really is when viewed from the implicitly superior standpoint. But let us dwell for a moment longer on that neatly turned phrase, 'the limit of classifying presumption'. The implication, from the superior vantage-point outside this commonplace, is that prisoners of the commonplace regard *all* efforts at classification as potentially presumptuous (the 'liberal' culture has to be parodied as incurably nominalist and resistant to any activity of concept-formation). But, braving the sarcastic edge of the phrase, we might ask: does Mulhern himself really believe there could be *no* need for a 'limit to classifying presumption'? It seems clear that he does not, at least where others are doing the classifying. But in that case, 'the individual person' is *bound* to be one possible source of such limits in relation to 'the social order', simply because social classifications, in however 'realist' a vein we construe them, are classifications of groups of individuals.

Whether literature constitutes a particularly fruitful source of such 'limits' in relation to public discourse is, I would agree, open to discussion, but there is nothing inherently naïve or obstructively nominalist or reprehensibly conservative in thinking that it may do. As mnemonics for the larger argument involved, one may cite two distinguished, if contrasting, cultural critics on the question. First, there is the celebrated observation of Lionel Trilling: 'To the carrying out of the job [of cultural criticism] literature has a unique relevance . . . because literature is the human activity that takes the fullest and most precise account of variousness,

---

39 'The Logic of Cultural Criticism', above, p. 109.

possibility, complexity and difficulty.'[40] And secondly, there is the less familiar remark by Roland Barthes, not normally regarded as a sharer of the commonplaces of any putative 'literary-liberal culture': 'Knowledge is coarse, life is subtle, and literature matters to us because it corrects this distance.'[41] Both these claims are, as I have already acknowledged, eminently contestable, but I recognize no standpoint from which they can be seen as *self-evidently* foolish or naïve, and nor, by the same token, do I see that one stands self-condemned as a result of being drawn to any such material that may indeed, in certain circumstances, help to set 'limits to classifying presumption'.

This point can also be addressed by reflecting on the import of what is merely a passing remark in 'Beyond Metaculture'. In the course of convicting Adorno of exhibiting a Marxist form of 'Kulturkritik', Mulhern points to the rather lofty tone of a sentence from *Prisms* in which Adorno was objecting to the ugliness and linguistically hybrid origins of the word 'Kulturkritik' in German, and he observes not just that the philology which Adorno implicitly appeals to is 'old school-room dogma', but also that 'the trope of discrimination is reminiscent of Henry James'.[42] I would not want to defend Adorno's expression of literary or intellectual taste here nor any general appeal to old school-room philological dogma, but I could not help wondering whether being 'reminiscent of Henry James' would in this context be so self-evidently undesirable. I found myself thinking, by contrast, that discrimination is at the heart of any worthwhile cultural criticism, and that

40   Lionel Trilling, *The Liberal Imagination: Essays on Literature and Society*, New York 1950, p. xv. Mulhern cites part of this passage in an earlier essay, finding Trilling's commitment to these qualities to be the essence of his 'feline liberalism' (*Present*, p. 90).

41   'La science est grossière, la vie est subtile, et c'est pour corriger cette distance que la littérature nous importe': Roland Barthes, 'Leçon' [Inaugural Lecture at the Collège de France], Paris 1978. The translation is taken from Michael Wood ('What Henry Knew', *London Review of Books*, 18 December 2003), who reads *science* as 'organized knowledge' and the idea of 'correction' as an optical one. In *A Barthes Reader*, ed. Susan Sontag, Richard Howard's translation is: 'Science is crude, life is subtle, and it is for the correction of this disparity that literature matters to us.'

42   'Beyond Metaculture', above, p. 56.

where discrimination is concerned James surely sets quite high standards. In making his own discriminations, he could certainly be precious and snobbish and much else besides, as, it seems, even Adorno could in his own way, but I would be sorry to think that, even when talking about cultural criticism in these rather un-Jamesian pages, he should only figure in this determinedly distanced way.

And that in turn led me to recall the exchange James had towards the end of his life with H. G. Wells, where Wells attacked the older novelist for a lack of social relevance (he memorably caricatured a James novel as 'a magnificent but painful hippopotamus resolved at any cost, even at the cost of its dignity, upon picking up a pea'). By contrast with this rarefied 'view of life and literature', Wells declared, 'I had rather be called a journalist than an artist'. It is, of course, the case that James did not tend to write much about the transformation of the social relations of capitalism, at least directly, and in those few novels that did take up some explicitly 'political' themes, such as *The Bostonians* and *The Princess Casamassima*, he hardly distinguished himself as an enthusiast for the 'progressive' causes of his day. But his magnificent response to Wells may nonetheless not be entirely irrelevant to the would-be cultural critic, brooding on the comparative fruitfulness of different routes to insight and understanding.

> But I *have* no view of life and literature, I maintain, other than that our form of the latter in especial [i.e. the novel] is admirable exactly by its range and variety, its plasticity and liberality, its fairly living on the sincere and shifting experience of the individual practitioner . . . For myself, I live, live intensely and am fed by life, and my value, whatever it be, is my own kind of expression of that . . . So far from [the art as opposed to the utility] of literature being irrelevant to the literary report upon life, and to its being made as interesting as possible, I regard it as relevant in a degree that leaves everything else behind. It is art that *makes* life, makes interest, makes importance, for our consideration and application of

these things, and I know of no substitute whatever for the force and beauty of its process.[43]

One does not have to subscribe to such aestheticism and subjectivism *au pied de la lettre* to feel that the 'plasticity and liberality' that James here invokes can indeed play a legitimate part in setting limits to classifying presumption.

III. Another Wave of the Wand?

We have travelled a long way from my initial brief review-essay on Mulhern's relatively short book. There I applauded the book's perceptive discussion of cultural studies and its identification of the unobvious continuities with some earlier forms of cultural criticism. But as the exchange has gone on, the nature of the differences between us has become clearer to me. I have come to feel that Mulhern over-generalized and even, dare I say, over-theorized his case: certain historically variable characteristics were turned into logically necessary features; other configurations were ruled illegitimate or impossible. The effect of his argument was to *eliminate* the possibility of legitimate cultural criticism: all such criticism is branded as 'Kulturkritik', a variant of metaculture; this is defined as an illegitimate attempt to take over the place rightfully occupied by politics. My role in this exchange has, therefore, principally been to lodge a protest: what we conventionally refer to as 'culture'—a piece of shorthand whose limitations are familiar—still provides, I have argued, a series of resources, idioms and perspectives that enable certain kinds of critical engagement with contemporary society. We do not have so many other resources of comparably enabling power, nor such imminent prospect of living in societies not in need of criticism, that we should hurry to rule this activity out of court just yet.

---

43   Henry James to H. G. Wells, 10 July 1915, in Philip Horne, ed., *Henry James: A Life in Letters*, London 1999, pp. 554–5.

The Primacy of Politics

Mulhern, by contrast, constantly asserts and reasserts the primacy of politics. But what, exactly, does that entail in the present case? The prize that, according to his account, politics and culture are vying for is 'authority'. The term appears in every key formulation of his argument: metacultural discourse is trying 'to supplant the authority of politics'; culture asserts 'a claim to authority over the social whole'; culture attempts to displace politics 'in the disputed plane of social authority'; in 'Kulturkritik' culture is the 'valid— because truly general—social authority'; 'the defining aim of what was to become Cultural Studies proper was to demystify the presumptive *authority* of Kulturkritik' (italics in original); and so on. I find something curiously univocal about these formulations: culture is always cast as some kind of illegitimate claimant to a throne rightfully occupied by politics because 'authority' is singular and indivisible. It may be helpful, instead, to import a distinction from classical sociology at this point. Here, put schematically, 'social authority' is understood as 'the probability that people will obey a command recognized as legitimate according to the prevailing rules in their society', whereas 'cultural authority' is understood as 'the probability that particular definitions of reality and judgements of meaning and value will prevail as valid and true'.[44] Where social authority is concerned, the sense of there needing to be in any given space an ultimate or final authority is immediately intelligible; this is, from another angle, the Weberian understanding of the state as the institution possessing a legitimate monopoly of force in a given territory. But with cultural authority, this is presumably not so: there is no 'final authority', only competing claims to authority.

The implication of Mulhern's critique of cultural criticism appears to be to assign to *politics* a legitimate monopoly of which 'definitions of reality and judgements of meaning and value will

---

44 I take these particular formulations from Paul Starr, *The Social Transformation of American Medicine*, New York 1982, p. 13; they may serve simply because Starr is here summarizing a body of classic sociological literature deriving from Weber and others.

prevail as valid and true'. Thus, at one point in *Culture/Metaculture*, in again invoking a distinction between 'substance' and 'form', he refers to a particular position as 'one of moral substance', which he glosses as meaning 'having to do with specific social interests and purposes'.[45] This courts, it seems to me, a restrictive and theoretically specified sense of 'moral', perhaps a sociologically reductive one. But it illustrates from another angle what is at issue: for Mulhern, questions about values, including the very large questions about how we should live, are 'empty' unless resolved into questions about 'specific social interests'. The clash of specific social interests, in its explicit and injunctive form, is the dynamic of politics, and politics, thus understood, is ultimately the arbiter of 'definitions of reality and judgements of meaning and value'. Such an understanding is, needless to say, by no means peculiar to Mulhern, but perhaps he has, from his earliest work onwards, shown a special concern with the ways in which in twentieth-century Britain fundamental political issues have been sublimated into or disguised as issues of culture, especially culture as mediated by literary critics.

In his most recent work, Mulhern chooses to label his own approach as that of 'cultural politics'. Does this perhaps represent some kind of theoretical Third Way, assigning primacy neither to politics nor to culture? Clearly not, I would say. As a way of approaching this question, consider the passage in the Introduction to *The Present Lasts a Long Time* where Mulhern distinguished his sense of 'cultural politics' from two extremes or caricatures: on the one hand, 'culturalism', 'the generic tendency of the liberal critical tradition', which 'asserts the moral primacy of culture over politics'; and on the other, 'instrumentalism', 'the error both fairly and falsely associated with socialist traditions, which elevates existing political priorities as the test of cultural legitimacy'.[46] But it should be noted that the terms in which this contrast is drawn silently introduce a triple asymmetry, so that a) 'the liberal tradition' is inescapably univocal, whereas 'socialist traditions' are allowed an appealing plurality; b) there is a part of these socialist traditions

---

45   Mulhern, *Culture/Metaculture*, p. 170, and 'Culture/Metaculture', above, p. 26.
46   Mulhern, *The Present Lasts a Long Time*, p. 6.

not 'fairly' open to this reproach, an extenuation not permitted to the liberal critical tradition; and c) the reproach in the case of the socialist traditions is narrowed to that of favouring 'existing political priorities', which then allows a true socialist politics to assert the moral primacy of some future form of social organization without incurring the charge of instrumentalism. Thus, a properly symmetrical version of the contrast would be: 'culturalism, the error both fairly and falsely associated with liberal traditions, which asserts the moral primacy of culture over politics', versus 'instrumentalism, the error both fairly and falsely associated with socialist traditions, which asserts the moral primacy of politics over culture'. Although these two positions are presented as the two extremes against which his own preferred 'cultural politics' is defined, the tilting of the contrast is only one indication of his actual leaning towards the latter member of the pair.

It is true that cultural politics, as he conceives it, may make use of the 'possibility' represented by the 'cultural excess', that is to say those aspects of meaning-bearing life which will always exceed or escape current political institutions and categories. But even so glossed, cultural politics is still politics, as his identifying it with 'the art of the possible' makes plain, as does his insistence that acknowledging the 'discrepancy', which is 'the space of cultural politics', is one of the marks of 'an emancipatory politics', here contrasted with 'any bourgeois political formula'.[47] So 'cultural politics' is not some third option which avoids giving priority to either politics or culture: it retains the primacy of politics, but seeks to exonerate itself, for the moment at least, from the charge of 'instrumentalism' by being open to the 'possibility' encoded in the cultural surplus. But always these possibilities are assessed by whether they point right or left; are you for us or against us; are you friend or enemy 'in final effect'? The evaluation is always 'in the first and last instance political'.[48]

---

47   Mulhern, *Culture/Metaculture*, pp. 174, 171, 162; *Present*, p. 7.
48   Mulhern, *Present*, p. 2. In this last example, he apparently (but, I think, only apparently) modifies the claim by saying: 'This evaluation of the historical probabilities is in the first and last instance political; but its underlying reasons find their premises in general theory, and are thus more than strictly political in their applications.'

One of the most tiresome and coercive clichés in current speech (as I have no doubt Mulhern would agree) is the phrase 'at the end of the day'. Among the sources of its offensiveness is the way in which it is so often used to rule that there always comes a moment when all that has gone before is rendered irrelevant: from that rhetorical vantage-point, all that matters is the outcome or reigning state of affairs at a posited moment of judgement, as in the logic of a game or war or contest of some kind. Of course, the implication may be false even in the case of those activities: there may well be more significant things about a game than the result (I hope Mulhern will not regard this as merely a 'convivial' English view). But a more telling objection to the common use of the phrase is the way it dismisses a whole range of important considerations in favour of the overriding significance of one particular kind of balance sheet. The metaphors are beginning to multiply, but one way to bring out the objectionableness of the cant phrase is to attend to the literal meaning lurking in the now more or less dead metaphor of 'the end of the day'. For the fact is that twilight or nightfall are only very small parts of the day indeed. Most of life is lived during the rest of the day, and night, and no one moment provides a summative perspective on all the others. Something similar, it seems to me, might be said about assigning overriding status to some political 'final analysis' or 'ultimate reckoning', whether projected to an unspecified point in future historical time or presented as the terminal point reached by theoretical analysis. Of course, we all have ethical or other commitments, and some can rightly claim to be more fundamental than others. But perhaps we need to resist the temptation to let them exercise a prematurely clinching power on the grounds of their privileged status when, ultimately, 'all is said and done'. 'All' never is said and done, and a political monism is no more appealing here than any other kind.

The Work of Criticism

Neither this essay nor any of my earlier contributions to this exchange are attempts to sketch a new theory of cultural criticism, not least because what I have to say is neither new nor a theory.

What I have been offering is, in the first instance, a protest, a protest against the elimination or closing down of a range of possibilities. Our dispute can at one level be understood as being not just between two vocabularies or ways of talking, but also between two different expectations about the level of abstraction required of such vocabularies, and perhaps even about how closed or self-consistent such vocabularies will be. It is for that reason that my responses have mostly taken the form of small-scale, local disagreements, now with this way of stating a case, now with that piece of labelling or classificatory preference, and so on. I well realize that the price I pay for this tactic, if one is thinking purely in terms of some kind of competitive or two-sided 'debate', is an apparent lack of focus or of theoretical force. But the tactic is, I believe, the appropriate expression of an underlying conviction about the value of persuasion and how persuasion takes place in these matters. That process seems to me more like contagion than like a mathematical demonstration; more like coming to enjoy someone's company than like losing at chess.

Mulhern's is undeniably a tidier intellectual world than mine, but the price of his impressively strenuous domestic regime may be that something valuable about cultural criticism has been tidied out of existence. Adapting Trilling's celebrated phrase, one may say that culture comprises the range of human activities that 'take the fullest and most precise account of variousness, possibility, complexity and difficulty', and for that reason cultural criticism is always likely to bring into play the kinds of consideration that are uncongenial to, or habitually neglected by, those more instrumental, pragmatic, aggregative processes which are nonetheless wholly necessary for running the world and getting its business done. Those general properties listed by Trilling may be encompassed in more than one way and alongside more than one set of political commitments. Equally, they are not constant or unambiguous goods in themselves, and not remotely the only goods. However, in that cluttered, medium-range, zone of engagement in which serious public debate takes place—well beyond the pragmatic hour-to-hour imperatives of action, but well short of the austere abstractions of systematic theory—any resources that help alert

us to variousness, and thus help to prevent our conceptions from
foreclosing the range of our perceptions, are worth having and
worth nurturing.

So, what I take myself to have been doing as I have moved
through what is by now a fairly extended series of these smaller,
local disagreements has been to engage in a practice, a practice
which I believe I share with Mulhern though he may not be willing
to accept this description of his part in the exchange. Criticism,
the elaboration and justification of perceptions about a given
object (which may, as in this case, include another writer's criticism), aims at persuasion. In any halfway interesting critical practice, the persuasion happens, as I have said, as much by example
and attraction as by propositional enforcement. In the course of
coming to be familiar with, perhaps eventually of coming to
inhabit and take active possession of, a way of talking, a reader
comes to share with the critic a number of discriminations, characterizations, enthusiasms, and aversions. Almost insensibly,
certain other ways of talking start to appear, in the given context,
as inexact, or exaggerated, or coarse-grained, or coercive, and so
on. It is always open to another voice in the conversation to challenge these perceptions, these judgements, these ways of talking,
but the new voice is nonetheless necessarily involved in a version
of the same practice. What we call 'theories' furnish powerful,
provocative, and wholly legitimate contributions to such conversations, often setting the standard in respect of definition of terms
and tightness of logical entailment. But such theories do not bring
the conversation to an end. Criticism makes use of the resources at
hand to call any such claims to finality into question, and when
readers—who are, after all, simply potential interlocutors temporarily given over to silence—find themselves drawn to object, to
agree, to admire, to doubt, to smile and to reflect, then the conversation has in practice already been moved on.

III

7

FRANCIS MULHERN

In the Academic Counting-House

Over the past decade, Stefan Collini has won widespread recognition at home and abroad for his incisive criticism of British higher education policy as it has developed since the 1980s, under Labour and Conservative governments indifferently. He has not been alone in this, of course: Andrew McGettigan has been tireless in unpicking the tangled threads of wishful thinking, cynicism, dogma and sheer recklessness that pass for rational financial policy and practice both in government and in the academic institutions themselves, while Helen Small—to take just one more notable example—has struck a contrasting emphasis, undertaking a critical appraisal of the current array of arguments in defence of an education in the humanities.[1] But Collini's record has been outstanding for its stamina and critical range: within the past decade there have been lectures to universities in Australia, Portugal, the US, Italy and the Netherlands, as well as several vintages of the UK system, addresses to conferences of various kinds, to unions and to a Westminster parliamentary committee, as well as articles for the print platforms where he has long been a familiar name, the *London Review of Books* and the *Guardian*. His range of topics extends from finance to axiology, bookends of a comprehensive engagement including the apotheosis of management and metrics, the follies of official research and teaching

---

1 Andrew McGettigan, *The Great University Gamble: Money, Markets and the Future of Higher Education*, London 2013; Helen Small, *The Value of the Humanities*, London 2013.

assessment, the status of students and the relative merits of different kinds of support for research and scholarly activity. From these diverse occasions, so many interventions in a single field of engagement, come the texts making up the bulk of his second book on the subject, *Speaking of Universities*.[2]

This has always been Collini's preferred mode of operation. He is a committed and skilled practitioner of the higher journalism, a master of what Bagehot in the middle 1850s characterized as 'the review-like essay and the essay-like review'.[3] Most of his books are focused compilations of such occasional pieces. The twin volumes *Common Reading* and *Common Writing*, from 2008 and 2016 respectively, are noteworthy cases in point. Between them, they contain thirty-seven chapters largely made up from thirty reviews of some sixty titles, the first offered as 'essays on literary culture and public debate', the second on 'critics, historians, publics'. They are evidence of enviable productivity and of the freedoms inherent in this prose form, even if those subtitles seem a little strained, not quite equal to their role in containing the miscellaneity within. Collini's intellectual histories lean towards portraiture rather than conceptual schemes: he has a liberal's suspicion of 'the pretensions of a full-blown ism' and so of what is pejoratively called 'labelling'—of others as well as himself.[4] At the same time, he is wary of the kind of history that provides the occasion for many of his essays—biography, which normally privileges the detail of an individual life over social-structural conditions—while showing what may be done in the frame of the genre with a virtuoso one-sentence exercise in the cultural stratigraphy of the subject, in this case the conservative historian Arthur Bryant:

> The figure whom Britain's cultural and political establishment had gathered to honour in Westminster Abbey in the 1980s had

---

2   Stefan Collini, *Speaking of Universities*, London 2017, hereafter SU. The first was *What Are Universities For?*, London 2012.

3   Stefan Collini, *Common Reading: Critics, Historians, Publics*, Oxford 2008, p. 223, hereafter CR.

4   Collini, 'Rolling It Out', CR, p. 31.

sustained into the 1950s a relation with a public defined in the 1920s and 1930s while writing in the manner and with the confidence of an Edwardian man of letters who in turn was striving to emulate the achievements of Victorian historians.[5]

Collini's Bryant is the 'historian as man of letters', and Collini himself is the historian as writer, self-consciously working with a rhetorical palette more varied than that of conventional scholarly discourse. Playful as well as 'pin-striped', his critical resources include all the ranges of mockery from mischief-making to satire. It is striking, too, how often his texts are shaped by a single presiding metaphor. Cyril Connolly is associated, not for the first time, with fine food and wine. The historian A. L. Rowse's writing habit appears akin to dipsomania: 'It hardly comes as a surprise to learn that he was a teetotaller: he didn't need it.' And Stephen Spender, as editor of the CIA-backed *Encounter*, emerges as a self-deceiving cuckold.[6]

Not too much should be made of that inevitable element of miscellaneity, however. Collini's historical coordinates have been constant over time: his field is English intellectual culture in the nineteenth and twentieth centuries, with strong leanings towards historical and literary thought—and occasional excursions to the US, as in his treatments of Edmund Wilson and Lionel Trilling. And within that field, a particular concern has been critical resistance to 'declinism', which Collini regards as a fixation of the culture. He has recently devoted a book-length study—originally the Ford Lectures given in Oxford in 2017—to this topic, arguing that English literary criticism as it took shape in the first half of the twentieth century was in effect a kind of cultural history, and one governed by declinist assumptions, a redoubt of 'the nostalgic imagination' and, as some would more bluntly judge, a 'misplaced cultural imperialism'.[7] The general thesis, in its broadest terms,

---

5   Collini, 'Believing in England', CR, p. 137.
6   Respectively, 'On Not Getting On with It', 'Disappointment' and 'Believing in Oneself', CR (the quoted matter is at p. 117).
7   Stefan Collini, *The Nostalgic Imagination: History in English Criticism*, Oxford 2019, p. 206.

will be familiar to many readers but has never been elaborated in such fine detail or with the same archival support. However, the book was a long time in the making, and years before the lectures were given, Collini had opened a second critical front. Declinism was no longer the main object of engagement, which was now something like its opposite: a thoroughly modern and thoroughly destructive programme of 'reform' of the Anglo-British higher education system—no decline this time, and not so much a fall as a wanton felling.

Measuring Up

The changes have not been uniformly negative. In the past three decades, universities have tripled in number (from 46 to 140-plus), while the student population has grown at double that rate (from around 350,000 to more than two million), and Collini is unequivocal in his support for this as 'a great democratic gain'.[8] However, he adds, over the same period of time 'the whole ecology of higher education in Britain has been transformed' in ways that the expansion of the system did not itself require: 'Most of the procedures governing funding, assessment, "quality control", "impact" and so on that now occupy the greater part of the working time of academics were unknown before the mid-1980s.' Norms of governance have been revised to promote 'top-down control' by 'senior management teams' at the expense of 'vestiges of academic self-government'. The core functions of the universities have been discursively refashioned as the elements of a business, to be run as such—or as organizations of that kind are thought to be run. In a complementary reform, the most widely known of them all and not merely another case of the pervasive linguistic programming of the period, students have been recast as customers: the consumers in the academic marketplace, financed now by a government loan scheme rather than grants from general taxation, and bent on value for money. For many of the universities, this will be a salutary discipline, the official reasoning goes: direct financial support

---

8   SU, p. 24. The figures are Collini's.

for teaching has been discontinued or reduced to a top-up, and success in the resulting competition for fee-paying students is now essential, with predictable gains in quality over time. For others, it is an opportunity. By 2013, more than half of the institutions validated as fit to receive government-funded fee income—and operating at significantly lower levels of regulation—were private, 'for-profit' as well as 'not-for-profit', with the latter sometimes the former trading in organizational disguise. In that year too, thanks to the intensive cultivation of emerging student markets in Asia and elsewhere, higher education ranked as the UK's seventh-largest 'export industry'.[9] In the space of a generation, higher education in the UK has been remade, and, under most pertinent headings, remade for the worse. The workings of the process, as recounted, analysed and assessed in what remains, for all its singularity of emphasis, a very diverse book, call for reading in detail, not least among those for whom this dismal British history may not yet presage a confirmed future; a critical report, in contrast, may best be framed in summary and correspondingly general terms.

The central term in Collini's critical account—its governing negative—is *metrics*, meaning 'the currently favoured, but actually doomed, endeavour to translate informed judgements of quality into calculable measures of quantity, and then to further reduce those quantitative proxies to a single ordinal ranking' in one of the league tables that have proliferated since the 1980s, becoming an obsessional focus of attention and effort throughout the system.[10] There is no doubting the ascendancy of quantitative measures in the evaluation of goals, purposes and achievements, including, increasingly, as a negative corollary the fading of considerations that are not amenable to quantifying procedures. But the objection cannot be to quantitative methods as such. That would be naïve, and misplaced as well, given the central role of quantification in

---

9   In the academic year, 2019–20, the number of Chinese students enrolled in UK universities rose to 120,000 and in one university alone—Liverpool—accounted for 20 per cent of the student body.

10   SU, p. 57.

necessary processes of administration and assessment. (After all, Collini's general wording would be a fair description of the process of aggregating, say, two dozen academic 'judgements of quality' to produce a final degree classification, each class itself internally ranked.) What is objectionable is the ascendancy of quantifiability as a threshold condition of relevance and admissibility, a species of transcendental reductionism in the plane of all that *Speaking of Universities* upholds as 'judgement'. We need look no further than the familiar, degraded world of academic research. Scientific and scholarly projects do well in these times to internalize the definitions, priorities and timescales of the Research Excellence Framework (REF, the sometime Research Assessment Exercise, first run in 1986), as a main condition of finding institutional support. Reputation—the regard of peers and of serious audiences—is a frothy index of achievement if it cannot be captured in scores and tables. League tables generally don't only reduce particular and distinct activities to a single numerical scale; they offer perverse compensation by generating distinctions that may not be detectable in working reality. Ten or fifteen institutions may differ within the space of 1–2 per cent, but the visual code of the table—equally spaced differentiation in the vertical plane—renders such trivia grave and lapidary, carves them in stone.

The quantities that matter most are financial, and the leading tendency now and in the relevant future is one of second-order quantification, or financialization. In the first stage of quantification, concrete intellectual purposes, practices and achievements are reduced to countable things—REF scores, league-table outcomes, external funding successes. In the second stage, the scores themselves are transcoded as money, which then comes to function as the substance of planning and evaluation. In prevailing conditions, as financial pressures become even more intense, the obvious danger in this is that financial promise serves as a privileged index of academic worth; fundability becomes the decisive validity test. The financial targets bring forth the concrete academic choices. Is this scholarly work REF-aligned and is it well placed to attract external income? If not, then switch to work that honours these desiderata. Follow the money ... In Collini's appropriately Marxian phrasing, 'The true use-value of scholarly labour can seem to have been somehow squeezed out; only the exchange-value of the commodities produced, as measured by the metrics, remains.'[11]

This fetishism is the principal count in Collini's indictment of the prevailing culture of mismeasurement, but not the only one. A second is that even in their own deforming terms, these operations may not be measuring what they claim to. The notion of research 'impact' offers a simple illustration. As defined, this would-be metric rules out consideration of the scientific or scholarly value of a piece of research to colleagues and students and its potential interest to wider, non-specialist audiences to whom it may be disseminated—'the public', or publics, as Collini prefers. What is left to appraise, then, as social 'impact', is probably not evidence of research quality at all but a record of 'extrinsic', mainly economic matters that may or may not be socially significant but are in any case contingencies incidental to the research itself. The Teaching Excellence Framework, which ranks institutions gold, silver or bronze, is an even plainer case: of the seven metrics it applies, including such compelling indicators of pedagogic excellence as graduate earnings, none bears on actual teaching.

These convergent processes have favoured a progressive abstraction of university functions, and the labour of perfecting and defending them has led to the development of an equally abstract organizational stratum of leader-managers. The tendency has been uneven, across what is a very diverse university system, but all one way. In a classic process of bureaucratization, institutional power becomes concentrated in a specialized layer of functionaries, at the expense of norms of policy-making and management which, if not altogether democratic, have been nevertheless more inclusive and collegial in character. This involves the weakening or abolition of such familiar conventions as fixed-term tenure in positions of responsibility and rotation of post-holders along agreed lines, and the extension of a

---

11   Ibid., p. 152.

contrasting principle of permanence ever further downwards from the top, to the point where not only faculty deans but also their specialized lieutenants (the standing committee chairs of yesteryear) and even heads of department come to be appointed from among those who look to these roles—or at least accept them—as strategic career choices. The right of return to ordinary duties is suspended, and for the hesitant, a change of contract may burn the boats. The emergence of this managerial stratum is assisted by restructuring processes that it in turn has facilitated, as faculties and schools are configured and reconfigured for reasons having more to do with finances and personnel than with academic considerations. The progressive rarefaction of management roles accentuates the old tendency, always latent in the division of organizational labour, to loosen the ties between post-holders and the academic population. The representative dimension of academic management fades from view—not in the stricter democratic sense, which may not have applied anyway, but in the sense of shared professional intuitions and ethos. Indeed it may not have been there to begin with, for a career manager, unlike a senior colleague taking a turn in a necessary position of responsibility, may come from anywhere in the system. There are deans in post today whose most advanced academic qualification is an MBA in higher education management.

Ideas of a University

So, one abstraction manages the university workforce by the light of another abstraction, with the aim of optimizing market share. The gilding of graduate earnings as an index of teaching quality is in its way an epitome of the general remaking, as Collini understands it. Together with such priceless data as the results of annual National Student Surveys, it signals the transformation of the student population into a flock of consumers in search of good value and an appreciable long-term return on their investment. As such, they have a strategic role to play, dynamizing the universities, with 'their archaic structures of self-government, their gentry-professional ethos and their blinkered devotion to useless knowledge'—all 'leftovers from an earlier history'.[12] Collini may be allowed the bitter edge in his voice. And yet this is not a narrative of decline, rather an angry counterpoint in a narrative of culmination, or—not to scant the sarcasm—fulfil-ment, in which, omelettes being what they are, eggs must be broken. 'Universities and research', Collini writes, 'have come increasingly under the aegis of bodies whose primary concerns are business, trade and employment.'[13] Such phrasing cannot help but sound a wrong, *ci-devant* note, it has to be said, however well-founded the observation itself. But elsewhere he speaks in terms that cannot be managed into the past. The 'unstated aim' of this wholesale remaking of higher education is 'to convert universities into market-driven corporations that are governed by the finan-cial imperatives of global capitalism'.[14] This purpose has been shared by Conservative and Labour governments, and is sustained by something more powerful than either: 'the drive by capital and its markets to mould human experience to its will', which 'is hardly going to lessen'.

Collini's sentence continues: 'and so neither will the flickering and uncertain recognition that universities are one major expres-sion of a still-valuable ideal of the open-ended search after fuller understanding that is not wholly governed by that economic logic'.[15] He is referring to writing in the genre of 'the Idea of a University' (the title of John Henry Newman's classic work, from the early 1850s), to which he now makes his own contribution. What is the idea and how can it be defended? To begin with, 'idea' is probably a mistaken choice of word, as in truth 'university' may also be, both of them being vulnerable to essentializing elabora-tions that Collini takes pains to forestall, insisting always on the historical character, the diversity of the institutions so designated, from the High Middle Ages to the present. 'But I do wonder', he reflects, 'whether we may not be approaching a point where our

---

12 Ibid., p. 157.
13 Ibid., p. 95.
14 Ibid., p. 147.
15 Ibid., p. 85.

usage of terms such as "universities" and "higher education" may . . . be best understood as the deployment of an inherited vocabulary without the underlying assumptions that for a long time made sense of it.'[16] Across the long century running from the emergence of the modern European university in the early nineteenth century to the expansionary wave of the three decades after the Second World War—the stretch of time from Humboldt to Robbins—'there is a recognizable family resemblance', a continuity of thinking:

> the idea that the university is a partly protected space in which the search for deeper and wider understanding takes precedence over all more immediate goals; the belief that, in addition to preparing the young for future employment, the aim of developing analytic and creative capacities is a worthwhile social purpose; the conviction that the existence of centres of disinterested enquiry and the transmission of a cultural and intellectual inheritance are self-evident public goods.[17]

But the experience of growth was misleading, an Indian summer that came to an end once the long post-war boom had subsided and inclement weather set in. Looking back from a distance of a further thirty years, Collini sounds more tentative than he need be or should be: 'We may be witnessing the shift from the university as shaped by the social-democratic era to the university as reflecting the era of the politics of market individualism.' In these conditions—and referring specifically to the humanities disciplines—he writes, there can be no realistic expectation of continuing benefit 'from the older kind of deference to the ideals of "culture"'.[18] Recalling the portmanteau name of an earlier movement of voluntaristic class purism, we might call the new order Marketcult.

---

16   Ibid., p. 155.
17   Ibid., p. 156.
18   Ibid., pp. 229–30.

Terms of Resistance

Collini is 'not optimistic' about the short-run prospects of a political counter-movement, and is certainly not dreaming of a return to the conditions of *les trente glorieuses*. (Indeed, it might be said that his fallback acceptance of a graduate tax as a second-best funding mechanism—his first preference being provision from progressive general taxation—already marks a concession to the prevailing view that university education is primarily an individual good rather than a necessary and desirable collective investment.) His immediate priority is resistance of the kind announced in his choice of mottoes.

The first, from Orwell's 'Politics and the English Language', is a call to arms against the 'invasion' of 'ready-made phrases'. Collini's title is exact: his book is about 'speaking', about the discourse that has been devised and propagated in the UK over the past thirty or more years as the one and only valid way of seeing universities today. His target is 'the language of the company report, with its relentlessly upbeat account of productivity, income streams, commercial partnerships and international ventures', leaving us with 'no way to distinguish the activities of universities from those of the business corporations in whose image they are being remade'. He is unrelenting in his mockery of the wooden, word-of-the-year formulism of the academic bureaucracy—the 'deliverables' that seldom refer to lectures or babies, 'excellence' meaning not outstanding but, roughly, up to scratch, and so on— and at times hilariously so, as when he announces 'our old friends Robust and Transparent, the Rosencrantz and Guildenstern' of this 'HiEdBiz' boilerplate.[19] The justifying function of universities, Collini maintains, is not their contribution to economic growth or the confused 'democratic' goal of 'social mobility' or any other 'immediate or instrumental purposes'. However, this must not be mistaken for a claim of academic exemption from ordinary 'usefulness'. That criterion is in reality highly diverse in its indication, and always context-dependent; and the familiar

---

19   Ibid., p. 166.

contrast of knowledge 'for its own sake' is arguably a misdescription of the various motivations that may be at work, singly or more often in combination, none of them really comparable to the ideal distillations of *l'art pour l'art*:

> A better way to characterize the intellectual life of universities may be to say that the drive towards understanding can never accept an arbitrary stopping point, and critique may always in principle reveal that any currently accepted stopping point *is* ultimately arbitrary. Human understanding, when not chained to a particular instrumental task, is restless, always pushing onwards, though not in a single or fixed or entirely knowable direction.[20]

That sudden uplift in register in the passage from the first sentence to the second is telling. This is an idealized vision, the university's 'best self'. The 'chains' in the concessionary qualifying clause are presented in the form of their absence, that is wishfully; but the mundane limitations for which they stand as proxies are nonetheless real and even integral to the ordinary pursuits of the academic institution, including its more advanced work. Training, the transmission of established understanding, is a much bigger part of what universities do than such formulations allow, not least in the UK, where the emphasis on undergraduate teaching has always been strong; Sartre's faux-intellectual 'technicians of practical knowledge' are in evidence everywhere, including those quarters where an etiquette of detachment prevails.[21] Yes, intellectual inquiry is an adventure, but its fruits may be bankable assets to be protected against all comers, and no longer in the spirit of the early work; and besides, can there be a sustainable intellectual practice without its moment of dogmatism? Senior managers have no monopoly of the 'ready-made phrase'.

---

20   Ibid., pp. 233–4.
21   Jean-Paul Sartre, 'A Plea for Intellectuals', in *Between Existentialism and Marxism*, London 1974, p. 237.

The second motto, from T. S. Eliot, inscribes the call to discursive resistance in an extended narrative:

> If we take the widest and wisest view of a Cause, there is no such thing as a Lost Cause because there is no such thing as a Gained Cause. We fight for lost causes because we know that our defeat and dismay may be the preface to our successors' victory, though that victory itself will be temporary; we fight rather to keep something alive than in the expectation that anything will triumph.

This show of tragic resolve is not altogether incongruous in its new setting, even if it is hardly characteristic Collini. But the more important feature of the passage is that it announces an inter-generational theme that recurs in *Speaking of Universities*, coming forward at the finish as a crowning argument. On its first appearance this marks the extended temporal aspect of the general reality of academic interdependence, which is also spatial, across institutional and national borders.[22] In its final, fullest statement, the inter-generational reality has come into its own and acquired the force of an ethical imperative. Interdependence through time complicates the idea of ownership, so that:

> If there is any value in reflecting from time to time on the unanswerable question of who the university belongs to, perhaps it lies in this—in reminding us, amid difficult political and financial circumstances, that we are only the trustees for the present generation of a complex intellectual inheritance that we did not create, and which it is not ours to allow to be destroyed.[23]

Movingly spoken—though 'inheritance' is too eirenic, misleadingly consensualist, as a description of the academic archive, which is a radically conflicted thing, and this prompts an associated objection to the form of Collini's argument, whose *locus*

---

22 SU, p. 45.
23 Ibid., p. 244.

classicus is Edmund Burke on the question of the French Revolution. In Burke's reasoning, the 'partnerships' that constitute the social bond are of a family character, such that inheritance is a contract of a special kind. Society, he wrote,

> is a partnership in all science; a partnership in all art; a partnership in every virtue and in all perfection. As the ends of such a partnership cannot be obtained in many generations, it becomes a partnership not only between those who are living, but between those who are living, those who are dead, and those who are to be born.[24]

With due allowance made for the legal niceties of bequeathing and inheriting, this logic, with the tendentious metaphor that facilitates it, is nevertheless fallacious. There cannot be partnership between the living, the dead and the unborn, because the living alone have agency in the here and now, have the capacity to make and execute decisions. They have no partners, if not one another. But Burke's advocacy was intended precisely to invalidate that partnership, to ward off a democracy of the living in the name of inheritance as mortmain—which he extolled as 'ten thousand times better than choice'. It hardly helps Collini's cause to see responsibility and choice so fatally polarized. This is a sword that turns in the hand, a conservative device that cannot so easily be made to serve progressive purposes, and need not be. At the level of basic assumptions, the fact of radical social interdependence— which always includes inter-generational relations—is surely sufficient to undermine the rationale of academic Marketcult and found the case for an open, cooperative public university system. However, the appeal to the objective socialization of life remains a long way short of a developed politics of reconstruction. The decades of neoliberal reform have seen the whole system called into question, and the echoes of that questioning outlive the immediate occasion. In refusing—correctly—the reductive,

---

24 Edmund Burke, *Reflections on the Revolution in France*, London 1968, pp. 194–5.

deforming logic of *homo oeconomicus* and the professional pragmatism it fosters, and at the same time—again correctly—discour-
aging any expectation of deference to received ideas of cultural
precedence, Collini leads his readers towards exposed ground, a
field of inescapable choices.

A Social-Democratic Turn?

This is unmistakably a critique from the left, plainly anti-capitalist
in its condemnation of the prevailing social and economic inequal-
ities and insistent on their stubborn, structural character. As such,
it calls for two related comments, the first of them retrospective
and in an obvious respect personal. Some sixteen years ago, in the
course of an exchange with Collini in *NLR*, I used the term 'quietist' in characterizing the 'cultural criticism' he was defending
against my general critique of 'metacultural discourse', 'a variation' unpersuaded by calls to political engagement, leaning rather
to the private sphere in its norms and priorities of evaluation.[25]
However much merit there may have been in this reading of the
texts then in question, I was too quick to infer a general politics
from the sensibility inscribed in them.[26] It soon became evident—
if it was not already apparent to someone more fully informed—
that as a rounded characterization of Stefan Collini as writer and
intellectual presence the judgement of quietism was mistaken. By
a satire of circumstance, it happened that, just as my text appeared,
late in 2003, he was writing 'HighEdBiz: Universities and Their
Publics', his scathing response to the Blair government's White
Paper *The Future of Higher Education* and an early landmark in
what became a marathon of public activism.[27]

However, a more nearly accurate, discriminating and telling
characterization may be available. It begins by broaching the question of Collini's placing on the spectrum of the left inclusively
understood. A standard summary would leave him somewhere on

25 'The Logic of Cultural Criticism', above, pp. 113–14.
26 In particular, ' "No Bullshit" Bullshit', on Christopher Hitchens.
27 Reprinted in CR.

the left wing of social democracy, trenchantly critical of capitalism and its thought-world: his rejection of economic 'growth' as
the obvious paramount good in policy-formation and of electoral
pragmatism as the highest form of political leadership marks his
distance from the nostrums of today's centre-left.[28] Yet the critical
target of his preferred 'Socialism' (so styled, upper case) is precisely
'unfettered' capitalism, which must be 'tamed' but not necessarily
put down, it seems.[29] Whether this qualification is grounded in
principle or historical judgement or simply a trained habit of
reservation, the indicated category would indeed be social democracy. But this is a greatly distended term, which over the past
century has accumulated meanings extending from reformist
strategies for the abolition of capitalism to the post-labourist
neoliberalism of the Blair years. Borrowing again from Sartre, we
might object that while Collini may be a social democrat, not
every social democrat is Stefan Collini.[30] A finer characterization
would take a simpler route, passing once more by way of the
theme of 'declinism' and Collini's vocal resistance to it.

The canon of English declinist thought is mainly literary—we
need think only of Eliot's modern 'dissociation of sensibility' or
Leavis's 'technologico-Benthamite' threat to cultural 'continuity',
which is itself one of many catastrophist accounts of the Industrial
Revolution—but the discourse of decline has been pervasive, as
Collini gives us to consider, not in his own words but those of E.
H. Carr, to whom he devotes an appreciative essay: 'The seat of
the most profound intellectual pessimism is to be found in Britain',
Carr wrote, for 'nowhere else is the contrast between nineteenth-
century splendour and twentieth-century drabness, between
nineteenth-century superiority and twentieth-century inferiority,

---

28   See his incisive treatment of the Labour grandee Roy Jenkins, 'Politician-
Intellectuals?', in *Common Writing: Essays on Literary Culture and Public Debate*,
Oxford 2016.

29   See for example the discussion of R. H. Tawney in his *English Pasts*, p. 190,
hereafter EP.

30   The original subject of the epigram was Paul Valéry: Jean-Paul Sartre, *The
Problem of Method*, London 1963, p. 56.

so marked and so painful.'[31] The condition is deep-laid, and ineluctably political—Eliot's summarizing term for everything he stood against was 'Whiggism', and Collini, like the more down-right William Empson before him, is not having it. 'The Whig Theory of History is the correct one,' Empson had written, 'and it is remarkable that the book given that title offers no single reason to think otherwise, being merely a fashion report of some High Table giggles.' Collini expands:

> Empson retained a wider optimism than was fashionable among the literary elite of the day that science, secularism, liberty and the social-democratic state were advancing on a common front . . . [His] sturdy liberal convictions made him a telling critic of all forms of cultural pessimism.[32]

That collocation of terms does less than full justice to Empson's socialist convictions, which underwrote his demonstrative public solidarity with the Chinese Revolution, and the phrasing—the date is circa 2006—sounds Whiggish indeed. But it gives the coordinates of Collini's political orientation.

A Liberal-Socialist Line

Collini's writing unites a 'progressive' politics (his own term) with a cultural liberalism that valorizes the historic archive as a critical reserve, amorphous in the positive sense that its valences may shift from one occasion to another, allowing renewals of perception and valuation—and radically eclectic in another perspective, as his choice of mottoes suggests: Eliot and Orwell for *Speaking of Universities*, Henry James, Nietzsche and Scholem for other volumes. An 'idealized conception of a university' is one locus of this living resource, the 'company' as which he is wont to model the authors he finds sympathetic. Collini's personalist commitment, to call it that, is to intellectual history

---

31   'The Intellectual as Realist', CR, p. 173.
32   'Smacking', CR, pp. 105–6.

as something more or other than 'history of ideas'. This cultural liberalism is a formative condition of his kind of 'Socialist' politics, however exactly they might be specified: social democracy, perhaps, but the more telling description would be 'liberal-socialism'.

The term comes out of the history of the Italian left in the 1920s, when it was coined by Carlo Rosselli to define a variety of reformism breaking with the intellectual inheritance of the Second International, committed to the goal of socialism but also, and crucially, to liberal institutional values, means and goals. Rosselli's main political inspiration was the British Labour movement, in which connection not many will immediately be put in mind of cultural liberalism: Labour's historic 'liberalism' was mostly a matter of constitutional inertia. But there was at least one Labour intellectual to whom the description 'liberal-socialist' applied: the *Tribune*-supporting Arnoldian Richard Hoggart. Here was the specular opposite of a kind of social-democratic cultivation sometimes called 'hinterland', the reserved area in a busy public life. Politics, in Hoggart, was a necessary but secondary consideration to be rendered, finally, in moral terms, the terms of a 'heritage' that was in an obvious sense a shared resource and yet—Collini's words—'how individual, almost private'.[33] This self-sublimating public discourse has something like ancestral status for Collini. He has written about Hoggart, the writer and critical observer of the common life, with real warmth and admiration. The idea of affiliation may over-interpret the suggestions of the prose, but they are there, and his closing words (he has been reviewing *Townscape with Figures*, from 1994) are an act of canonization:

> Hoggart's natural home is not with that international company of cultural analysts, literary theorists, and assorted academic superstars who are today's most familiar intellectuals. He belongs, rather, to an older family, one with strong local roots and some pride in ancestry; his forebears include Ruskin and

---

33 'Critical Minds', EP, p. 229.

Lawrence on one side, Cobbett and Orwell on the other. Richard Hoggart is an English moralist.[34]

The hyphen in 'liberal-socialist' is not a fixed value; the compound varies according to the exponent and the given situation. Hoggart was a declared 'once-born Socialist' who spent much of his working life in the higher levels of cultural policy and administration— an admirer of Orwell, indeed, but as his CV confirms, a dedicated and greatly respected member of the liberal service intelligentsia. Collini, on the other hand, remains averse to political self-classification, in a familiar liberal reflex, while conducting a public campaign worthy of Michael Kohlhaas against government higher education policy and the academic functionaries who mediate it. There is a suggestion of paradox in this distribution, which a difference of context goes some way to explaining. All organizations have their passages of crisis, but surely none of the many committees and boards that Hoggart served on, ranging from the *New Statesman* and the Royal Shakespeare Company to UNESCO and a London University college, suffered the kind of prolonged, system-wide convulsions that the UK's universities have borne over more than a generation—and these not as unintended consequences but as objects of policy. Hoggart retired from Goldsmiths to a long after-career as a writer just as that sequence of trials was beginning, in the earlier 1980s. For a like-minded academic some thirty years his junior, fidelity to the 'ideal' liberal university could not be a sequestered option, nor would it be served in the form of yet another narrative of decline: it was in the most down-to-earth sense bluntly, inescapably political.

---

34 Ibid., p. 230. Writing twenty-odd years later, Collini subjected Hoggart's *Uses of Literacy* to stringent examination for its part in the declinist culture of English literary criticism: *The Nostalgic Imagination*, pp. 138–55. But with all allowances made for the accumulated second and further thoughts of twenty years, concerning a body of writing spanning twice as long, the difference is not the plain contrast it seems to be. One treatment is an analysis of a book; the other is an evaluation of a man.

Academic Prospects

And yet even at its most trenchant, Collini's argumentation has remained—in spite of itself—somehow politically abstract, indicting a system and its culture, that of capitalism, but at a familiar, contemplative distance. The overmastering reality is a machine-like system that must be resisted in the name of an inherited grace: Eliot's theme of a cause that is never quite lost and never finally gained turns out to be no more than the prosaic truth of the matter. One apparent departure from this contemplative tendency was the open letter Collini wrote to Liam Byrne, a Labour MP and at the time (2013) the newly appointed opposition spokesperson on universities.[35] A Harvard MBA and energetic Blairite, Byrne was not the likeliest or most sympathetic of addressees, but he had given some sign of taking an interest in the cruces of higher education funding policy, and Collini moved to make his case. He urged an end to the abusive modelling of teaching and learning as a business transaction and to the loan scheme associated with it; a thorough review of research assessment procedures; and the creation of a government department adapted for the distinctive needs and purposes of universities and related areas of cultural and scientific activity. And there it rested. The letter was never sent, or published in any form until *Speaking of Universities*, where it appears in an appendix with the title 'Short Work'.

Short indeed, and in one politically decisive respect, short-weight. The measures Collini has proposed are unobjectionable—and in fact the first two featured in Labour's 2019 election manifesto—but the third and last of them, concerned to fortify the old principle of 'arms-length' government funding, illuminates a significant absence. There is no reference on this occasion to institutional politics, the *internal* management of university affairs, and specifically no mention of the bureaucratic degeneration of the past decades: the wholesale assimilation of the professoriat to a corporate 'senior management', the downward spread of permanent appointments in posts of responsibility, the remaking of

---

35   SU, pp. 272–5.

committees as 'teams', and the rest. It is not that Collini is indifferent to these developments, and it is true, of course, that such matters are not usually the concern of government—in this respect the arms-length convention may actually favour bureaucratic preferences—but they are not forbidden territory either. Besides, open letters are written to win the attention of a relatively mass readership, rather than the authority-figures to whom they are nominally addressed, and the core mass audience in this case would be academics, whose typical reaction in the face of all this has been, as Collini says, mere 'hand-wringing', or making the best of things as they are and seemingly must be. A generic anti-capitalist denunciation of the prevailing trends of the past thirty years is more likely than not to produce more of the same, or at most a high-minded abstention from the official linguistic decorum, for want of any point of collective political leverage. In this lies the importance of developing concrete demands, both local and general, aimed at limiting and reversing the advance of the academic bureaucracy. Without the coadjutant formation of that managerial stratum the marketization of university education would have been far more difficult, if not impossible, to achieve. What element of academic self-government may yet be saved or restored or even won will vary from place to place, and from one kind of institution to another. In no case can it be said with confidence that the odds are good, after Labour's electoral debacle in 2019 and at a time when the militant energies of the university teachers' union, never so great and already hampered by reactionary legislation, are engrossed in the elemental questions of pay, pensions, workloads, casualization and equality in work. But a collective effort on this front will be an indispensable part of the general struggle for a progressive renewal of the university system.

8

STEFAN COLLINI

The Naming of Parts

> It is one of man's most settled habits, when he meets with
> anything new and strange, to be unhappy until he has named it,
> and, when he has named it, to be for ever at rest.
>
> Walter Raleigh, *Shakespeare*[1]

What is the relation of intellectual work to political allegiances?
What is involved in developing viable forms of cultural criticism
on the Left that are not grounded in the Marxist tradition? How
can the discourse of 'culture' play its part in such criticism without ultimately leading to an alarmist or nostalgic displacement
of politics? Are invocations of 'complexity' and 'variousness'
doing real work in this criticism, or are they more often just self-
flattering disguises for incoherent eclecticism? What does 'liberal'
mean in contemporary Left discussion, and is it still a useful
label?

These questions are at the heart of the intellectual exchanges
that Francis Mulhern and I have been having (and will, I hope,
continue to have in some form or other). The present volume has
not been undertaken as a form of closure: it is—it can only be—a
progress report, a stock-taking prompted partly by Mulhern's
2016 book *Figures of Catastrophe*, partly by his assessment of
some of my recent work in his essay 'In the Academic Counting-
House', and partly by the forthcoming publication of a new

---

1   Walter Raleigh, *Shakespeare*, London 1907, pp. 17–18.

volume of his essays, *Into the Mêlée*.[2] For these as well as other
reasons, including an urge on my part to modify or move away
from some of my earlier formulations, I shan't attempt an overview or summary of our exchanges here, the main sequence of
which has anyway been quite widely discussed by others.[3]
Instead, I shall address Mulhern's recent work, attending particularly to the ways it bears on the recurrent themes of our long-
running exchange. I'll conclude with some brief remarks about
the topography of current intellectual debate and ask who gets to
name its constituent features.

Figures of Catastrophe and Into the Mêlée

Mulhern characterizes *Figures of Catastrophe* as 'the third part of
an unplanned, informal trio offering elements of a critical history
of metaculture, the discourse in which the principle of "culture"
speaks of itself and its general conditions of existence'—*The
Moment of Scrutiny* (1979) and *Culture/Metaculture* (2000)
coming retrospectively to constitute the first two parts.[4]
Substantively, all three books might be said to be haunted by a
wary suspicion that the legacy of Matthew Arnold has long exercised an unhealthy influence over too much English social thinking, with F. R. Leavis as its main avatar in twentieth-century
literary and cultural criticism, and E. M. Forster its defining representative in the novel. Overall, there is certainly nothing parochial

---

2 Francis Mulhern, *Figures of Catastrophe: The Condition of Culture Novel*,
London and New York 2016; Francis Mulhern, *Into the Mêlée: Culture/Politics/
Intellectuals*, London and New York 2024. I am grateful to Francis Mulhern and to
Verso for enabling me to see the typescript of this collection in advance of
publication.

3 For example, David Simpson, 'Politics as Such?', *New Left Review* 30,
November–December 2004, pp. 69–82; Jorge Myers, 'Entre la Kulturkritik y los
Estudios culturales: Un debate contemporáneo entre Francis Mulhern y Stefan
Collini', *Prismas: Revista de historia intelectual*, 2005, pp. 283–90; James Walter
Caufield, *Overcoming Matthew Arnold: Ethics in Culture and Criticism*, London
2012; Ji Kwan Yoon, 'The Poverty of Criticism: On the Mulhern–Collini
Controversy', *Journal of English Studies in Korea* 36, 2019, pp. 1–15; Bruce Robbins,
'Class, Culture and Killing', *Boundary 2*, vol. 47, no. 1, 2020, pp. 201–13.

4 Mulhern, *Figures*, p. vii.

about Mulhern's range of reading and concern, which are impressively international in the best *NLR* tradition, but the third part of the informal trilogy again puts 'the matter of England' at the heart of his critical work: 'The condition of culture novel as I have constructed its history here has been an English phenomenon.'[5]

Figures of Catastrophe is a condensed, powerful book—and correspondingly hard to summarize. It works with a notion of 'genre' understood as 'groups of texts sharing a distinctive topic or set of topics' as their dominant theme, and it proposes the existence of 'the condition of culture' novel as such a genre in English fiction. Mulhern identifies a sequence of a dozen works, running from *Jude the Obscure* and *Howards End* to Hanif Kureishi's *The Black Album* and Zadie Smith's *On Beauty*, as the main exemplars of this genre. In each of these books, he argues, we encounter attempts to invoke or deploy ideas of culture as, variously, stays against social decline, consolations for loss or absence in the present, antidotes to demotic self-assertion or popular unrest, and more. The controlling frame of the book is fiercely taxonomic, while the individual readings are rich in sharply observed detail and pointed decodings.

In relation to our continuing exchanges, the most salient feature of *Figures of Catastrophe* is its explanatory logic. The novels it discusses are said to be united in representing culture as somehow under threat from the uncultured masses, whether in the form of organized working-class movements or simply popular entertainments. 'Culture as principle', Mulhern writes, 'is an exclusive universal, a figure of discourse that produces and reproduces its own menacing other, an ideological power complicit with the social order that fosters the deformities it laments.'[6] The structure of this (characteristic) sentence implies that all its clauses are simply fuller elucidations of the meaning contained in the idea of 'culture as principle'. This idea, it is argued, is always doing ideological work. It ultimately bolsters the existing social order by conjuring up features of that order which are portrayed as

---

5   Ibid., p. 149.
6   Ibid., p. 155.

threatening, only to repudiate or overcome them in the name of culture itself. The character of the explanation seems to involve some kind of reciprocal relation between two elements or levels. On the one hand, the whole encounter between culture and its menacing other is represented as some phantasmagoric invention, the staging of a conflict that only exists because of culture's need to define itself against a threatening other. On the other hand, this happens because of actual developments in that social order, such that the existence or otherwise of organized working-class militancy has a causal priority when it comes to analysing the sequence of 'condition of culture' novels discussed in the book.

The intriguing implication here seems to be that the 'condition of culture' novel can only arise when the working-class 'threat' is merely latent or in abeyance, as, allegedly, in England from the late nineteenth century. At other times and places, such as England in the 1840s or France and Germany at the end of the nineteenth century, literature becomes more frankly descriptive of the overt class antagonisms of the day. It would seem to follow that novels accurately representing such conflict would *not* be subject to the same kind of symptomatic reading that Mulhern practises in this book, since there would be no 'displacement' involved. Thus, he says of the 'industrial novel' of the 1840s that in a period when 'the working class had massed under the revolutionary-democratic banner of the People's Charter, there was little scope for symbolic displacement'.[7] In other words, if there is one kind of explicit class politics happening in society, then novels don't need to encode it in any way—they straightforwardly describe it; but if politics takes other, less directly class-conscious, forms, then the ground is ready for Mulhern's 'condition of culture' novel to flourish, one in which fear of popular or working-class power is encoded or sublimated. It is precisely because of the alleged hegemony of a form of liberalism over the British working class at the end of the nineteenth century, rather than of any kind of revolutionary socialism as in some other European countries, that conflict had to take an oblique form in the fiction: 'that peaceable liberal meliorism found

---

7   Ibid., p. 153.

a voice for its compulsive counter-imaginings' by fretting that the ascendancy of a confident, prosperous, and vulgar working class was threatening to overwhelm culture.[8] These are the 'figures of catastrophe' of the book's title.

In such an account, the character of particular works of literature does seem to be locked into an extraordinarily tight relation with the fluctuations of popular politics. I am not here concerned to produce counterexamples that do not fit either part of this pattern, but rather to probe the character of the explanatory mechanism itself. Of course, writers respond to their times, but *how* they respond may not be wholly determined by those times, certainly not by just one feature of them. Do we, for example, understand anything better about *Howards End*, published in 1910, by learning that 'as late as 1914, Europe's oldest industrial working class was trailing all its comparable neighbours in the development of independent political representation'?[9] And anyway, why is the working class the privileged historical force in such stories? If one were looking for major forms of social conflict at the time Forster was writing, the struggle for women's suffrage and the clashes over Ireland would surely bulk as large. But it seems that for Mulhern these are not determinants of the character of the novels in the way that (sublimated) conflict between the working class and the bourgeoisie is. What shapes the development of a whole new genre is not what contemporaries may have experienced as the major forms of conflict, but rather the underlying class relations.

This seems to be, in essence, what Mulhern terms his 'Marxist formalism'. Where the adjective indicates a familiar explanatory framework, the noun goes beyond a conventional attention to form and signifies a taxonomic urge to identify and codify shared structural similarities underlying apparent multiplicity, an approach that gives *Figures of Catastrophe* some kinship with the intellectual impulses behind Structuralism. The goal in both cases is to uncover patterns which are characterized, and validated, as being 'deeper'—deeper than those 'surface' features which so much

---

8   Ibid.
9   Ibid., p. 154.

attract the eye of traditional literary criticism. This Structuralist affinity is expressed most obviously in the use Mulhern makes of the classificatory grids of A. J. Greimas, with their determining antinomies and matching tensions or resolutions. But the fact is that these grids are not simply given; they are not made up of indisputable or objective characteristics of the works themselves. At one point Mulhern fairly admits that the fruitfulness of this grid structure depends on the rightness of the critic's choice of terms to put in the main boxes to begin with. However, these terms can only be selected on the basis of a judgement about what the key themes of the novel in question are, so this does seem to concede that the would-be scientific character of the approach is dependent on the literary-critical acuity of the critic, and his or her choice of vocabulary, in the first place.

The approach works best with the most transparently allegorical novels, such as *Howards End* (surely the defining text for Mulhern's story) or Zadie Smith's *On Beauty*, its self-declared step-child. It feels most strained in the case of works of greater formal distinctiveness, such as Woolf's *Orlando* or Naipaul's *The Enigma of Arrival*, where so much that is interesting about their unusual generic properties escapes this deliberately Procrustean grid. More generally, this overriding taxonomic ambition makes the book, like so much of Mulhern's writing, both compact and spare. There is little literary criticism in the traditional sense, though Mulhern clearly has an acute ear. There is little of a biographical or contextual character, beyond the meta-historical framework of various forms of popular challenge to elite cultural dominance. And there is little reference either to other writers from the various periods or to the work of other critics. All this adds to an air of settled intellectual confidence: one task appears as self-evidently more important than any other; one approach claims to yield more fruit than any other. Other matters are not just omitted—they come to seem, by implication, superficial or inessential. Headquartered in this well-established base, Mulhern can then proceed to provide strong symptomatic readings of a dozen novels that illustrate what he claims is a distinctive genre.

The readings are attentive and in many respects persuasive, but

at times I do find myself wondering quite how much they owe to
the conceptual undergirding of a 'Marxist formalism'. No reader
of *Howards End*, for example, can miss the symbolism; indeed,
the somewhat clunky allegorical machinery is what so many critics
have held against the book. Or take Mulhern's reading of
Brideshead Revisited: the analysis is well done and typically
economical, but is it distinctive? Who could fail to register that
this is a book about loss, a book suffused with nostalgia and snob-
bery, a book that revels in the voluptuousness of its descriptions,
whether of old houses or fine wines or just the languor of youth
lolling away a hot summer in privileged ease. The threat represented by 'The Age of Hooper' hardly needs any decoding. The
idea that solace is sought in the aristocratic principle, in the continuity of the great house, and finally, tragically, in the practices of
a ritualized old religion, is clearly legible on the surface of the
novel. It is obviously of its time, written late in the Second World
War, suffused with a dread of the drab, levelling uniformity Waugh
feared was to come, and arguably (at a stretch) it does bear a
thematic resemblance to, say, *Howards End* or Ruth Rendell's *A
Judgement in Stone*, one of the minor novels that genuinely gains
from being considered alongside the more celebrated examples.
But, sharp though Mulhern's comments on Waugh's novel are,
they do not really seem to depend on any materialist presupposi-
tion, nor to issue in a reading that is significantly different from
those produced by critics not working under that dispensation.

That may not matter for Mulhern; for him the stress may fall on
the significance of the overall pattern, not the distinctiveness of a
particular reading. 'It is only in the light of methodical comparison that we can hope to leave familiarity behind and progress
towards a more adequate rational construction of the object in its
real individuality.'[10] This is a characteristic affirmation. At first
sight it might seem to describe an element in all forms of intellectual labour: we only grasp the true individuality of an object by
charting its resemblances to and differences from ostensibly similar objects. But in the context of Mulhern's project in *Figures of*

10   Ibid., p. 150.

Catastrophe, the passage signals something much more ambitious: in understanding and responding to a body of literature we need, it insists, to leave behind 'familiarity' and to build a 'more adequate rational construction' of the work which brings out its 'real' individuality. The contingent character of the individual books involved gives way to a rational construction, one which eliminates the contingency. The 'real individuality' that is thus brought out is real in a particular philosophical sense, a form of significance deriving from being assigned its place in a grid of concepts. The operation so described seems nearer to the Hegelian thinking of a 'concrete universal' than it does to traditional literary criticism.

This underlines one of the major differences between Mulhern's work and my own, even when, as has quite often happened, we are dealing with much the same material. One way to represent a basic contrast between our respective modi operandi would be to compare, once again, the different roles played by a form of 'characterizing'. This is, for me, one of the fundamental undertakings of all criticism and intellectual history. By it, I tend to mean that intensifying and thickening of a perception about a figure or a work through a kind of extended individuated description, rather of a kind I might give to someone else about a third party of our common acquaintance whom I have had special occasion to try to understand. Most of the vocabulary used will be that of ordinary human description and evaluation, but more extensive contextual and historical resources will be brought in to thicken the texture of the description. In an ideal world, such characterizing elicits from a reader or listener a form of recognition, a sense that something previously only half-noticed has been captured and displayed in an illuminating way.

Mulhern's form of characterizing begins by positing an underlying determining structure that sets aside irrelevant detail, a structure which is then, in turn, placed in a taxonomy of related but distinct structures, each given a historical genesis or location, so that the specific logic of its operation stands out, albeit understood as a unique instantiation of general properties shared among the range of relevant structures. Whereas some of my work

may be thought of as trying to establish a more intimate familiarity with the voices of past actors or the texture of past situations,
Mulhern's work usually involves a process of deliberate defamil-
iarization. His writing is a strenuous exercise in unsettling our
established idioms and judgements by redescribing them in terms
that present themselves as at once more abstract and more fundamental. Something of the sort is constitutive of all intellectual
work, of course: the quiddity of Mulhern's version of it in this
book (and here I do a little 'characterizing' of my own) lies in its
strong classificatory drive combined with a decisiveness about
what really matters, a combination that issues in a bracing uncon-
cern with, perhaps at times even intolerance of, the under-
theorized vocabularies of so much commentary and scholarship.

It is noticeable that Mulhern's work has returned again and
again to a particular period—roughly the first half of the twentieth century, and especially the inter-war years. This was, unavoid-
ably, the focus of *The Moment of Scrutiny*; the examination of the
tradition of Kultukritik at the heart of *Culture/Metaculture* is
grounded in the European critics of these decades; and the defining readings in *Figures of Catastrophe* are those that range from
Howards End in 1910 to *Brideshead* in 1945. It has long been
recognized that it was during these years that the clash between—
to take the terms in Leavis's polemical title—'mass civilization'
and 'minority culture' was experienced as being particularly
pronounced, but is that enough to account for Mulhern's continuing preoccupation?

I would hazard that at least part of the reason for this marked
stability in Mulhern's critical concerns is the old question of why
Britain in the twentieth century has been seen as escaping the most
overt forms of conflict between the working class and the bourgeoisie. As the 'first industrial nation', Britain seemed destined to
pioneer such conflict, but, so the argument runs, this was 'diverted',
partly by the development of a 'meliorist' working-class politics,
partly by a discourse of 'culture' that transposed such conflict to
another plane. Through the early and middle decades of the twentieth century, the continuing hegemony of traditional forms of
culture, associated with the upper and upper-middle classes,

helped to obscure the underlying reality of class relations. A properly radical 'cultural politics' (the term Mulhern chooses for his enterprise in *Culture/Metaculture*) should accordingly be devoted to demystifying the traditional claims of 'culture'.

I have put this case in deliberately stark terms; no one could deny that the actual texture of Mulhern's writing is always more sophisticated and nuanced than this. But it is, in its bare outlines, a familiar story, and in terms of immediate antecedents one can see resemblances to two classics of New Left thinking, Raymond Williams's *Culture and Society* and Perry Anderson's 'Components of the National Culture'. I have attempted to engage with their arguments at some length elsewhere, and I shall not repeat those analyses here.[11] Suffice it to say that in both these works there lurks an idea of culture as either compensatory or a form of displacement, the shadow-world into which class antagonisms are projected when they cannot be explicitly confronted in the present, an assumption that is especially evident in Mulhern's early writing. The imprint of those exemplars seems somewhat less legible in his more recent essays, yet it is ironic that Mulhern should emphasize the different trajectories in working-class politics in Britain compared to the leading European states as a way of isolating the distinctiveness of his genre in *Figures of Catastrophe*, when the character of the anxiety that defines that genre seems exactly the same as that which constitutes *Kulturkritik* in *Metaculture*—that is, a largely *Continental European* anxiety and tradition of response to it.

Turning to *Into the Mêlée*, it is noteworthy that over half the pieces in it are from the last decade, and these recent performances in the genre of the critical essay represent, in my view, Mulhern's writing at its very best. There are arrestingly fine pieces here on figures as different as Ferdinand Mount and Roberto Schwarz, on the stylish literary criticism of James Wood or the Brooklyn cool

---

11 For an extended reading of *Culture and Society*, see Collini, *The Nostalgic Imagination*, Oxford 2019, Chapter 6; for a critique of Anderson's classic essay, see Stefan Collini, *Absent Minds: Intellectuals in Britain*, Oxford 2006, pp. 175–83.

of the radical journal *n+1*. But as Mulhern explains in discussing his choice of title, the claim to be '*au-dessus de la mêlée*' has been the deforming fault of the tradition of cultural criticism (which he again prefers to render as 'Kulturkritik', unitalicized), 'a call to cultural service beyond the deforming pressures of everyday political and social strife', against which he asserts that 'there is no social location corresponding to this desire'; and so his own work understands itself to be wholly and frankly 'in' the mêlée. This seems immediately appealing, but does it perhaps too briskly elide the necessary distinctions? There have indeed been those who have represented themselves as being 'above' politics, and Mulhern's strictures against them are merited. But if it is claimed, as parts of our earlier exchanges may seem to suggest, that this applies to *any* form of self-described cultural criticism (my own included), then the claim does not seem justified. To assert, as I do, that there are things which cultural criticism can bring to debate that are not reducible to politics is not to position oneself as 'above' the mêlée. And anyway, why does politics get to define the 'mêlée' in the first place? Surely there are many 'everyday' things other than politics that go into making up the mêlée of life?

Moreover, Mulhern's knock-down rebuttal at this point rests on saying that 'there is no social location corresponding to this desire', but it's not obvious that the question is one of *social* location rather than, say, implied vantage-point or distance. Criticism necessarily involves some kind of 'standing back', observing, reflecting, and judging (in practice Mulhern's own essays are excellent examples of these procedures and their removed perspective). To that extent, all such critical writing can seem, through the ineluctable pressure of form, *au-dessus de la mêlée*. But that is no indictment of such writing; it is an acknowledgement of the logic of critical assessment, the unavoidable assumption of a 'removed' perspective, if only for the duration of the procedure.

I wonder if Mulhern, while obviously being familiar with this point, might also be made somewhat uneasy by it. The final sentences of *Into the Mêlée*, from the 2022 postscript to his *n+1* essay, are these:

'It is time to say what you mean' was the watchword [of the journal] in 2004. It would be echoed in the magazine years later, this time in the voice of the opposition journalist Natalia Tyshkevich in the early days of Putin's war on Ukraine, as she awaited her trial: 'The irony has fallen away completely . . . The jokes are over.'[12]

There is a clear performative force in ending thus. Up to the final pages, Mulhern has admired, and criticized, the literary inventiveness and variable registers of the magazine's most characteristic writing, but here, he seems to want to say (but not quite to say), we touch bottom. Enough already of the clever stuff: the questions now are 'Whose side are you on?' and 'What is to be done?', the emblematic questions of politics. It's that note of finality again, that at-the-end-of-the-day no-two-ways-about-it assertion of the inescapable. Yet in a way his whole essay up to this point brilliantly exhibits that what is valuable and interesting about *n+1* does not lie here.

It may be mischievous on my part to say that what we sometimes see in Mulhern's recent writing is a 'return upon himself', but there do seem to be moments where he, having been absorbed in the task of delicately discriminating and characterizing, suddenly recalls himself to his political purpose.[13] As I've already hinted, the features of *Figures of Catastrophe* that are so good are quite similar to the things that are so good about the best of traditional literary criticism. Part of what, in my view, makes Mulhern such an interesting writer, especially in his more recent essays, is his ambivalent attraction to the strengths of that form of writing and his ability to match it on its own ground. Indeed, were James Wood not the subject of the most recent essay in *Into the Mêlée*,

---

12   Mulhern, 'A Party of Latecomers' in *Into the Mêlée*, p. 30.
13   Matthew Arnold, in a phrase that has been much cited, spoke admiringly of Edmund Burke's 'return upon himself' in a passage in which Burke felt driven to adopt a position contrary to the whole tenor of his preceding argument about the French Revolution; see 'The Function of Criticism at the Present Time' [1864], in *The Complete Prose Works of Matthew Arnold*, vol. 3, ed. R. H. Super, Ann Arbor 1962, pp. 267–8.

'Caution, Metaphors at Work', one might begin to think parts of it were written by James Wood. Except that there is a characteristically Mulhernian move when he, disconcertingly, compares Wood to Lukács. Noting that both are constantly evaluative, Mulhern writes:

> But whereas Lukács's evaluations were grounded in an explicit and ordered understanding of historical actuality and possibility, Wood's have no comparable sanction, be it ethico-political or for that matter aesthetic . . . The appeal to 'life' and the really real can hardly fail to summon the spirit of a critic who goes unmentioned: F. R. Leavis. Yet even he, the 'anti-philosopher', rooted his Lawrentian vitalism in a romantic theory of modernity. His conviction of self-evidence was not self-enclosed.[14]

'Grounded in an explicit and ordered understanding of historical actuality and possibility'. This functions as a *rappel à l'ordre*, a rapping of literary criticism over the knuckles. It is all very well, he implies, for Wood to go on about 'serious noticing' and to be so gifted at doing it, but there is no basis for his critical judgements unless they are grounded in some equivalent to 'an explicit and ordered understanding of historical actuality and possibility'. But his implication that Wood's appeals to 'self-evidence' are 'self-enclosed' in some damning way is a charge without substance. All literary criticism involves something like an appeal to self-evidence because it is trying to persuade the reader to see what is already there, to inhabit a text in the way the critic does. The procedure does not gain in validity by trying to claim an external warrant in a present of human exploitation or a future of human emancipation.

One might even see an irony in the fact that Mulhern, severe censor of anything that looks as though it claims to stand 'outside' the mêlée, asserts the need to ground criticism in something that clearly stands 'outside' itself. Surely it is Wood who, from this point of view, is 'in' the mêlée, the mêlée that is life, and Mulhern

---

14   Mulhern, 'Caution, Metaphors at Work', in *Into the Mêlée*, p. 7.

who is appraising from afar (very afar, if one takes the phrase about 'an ordered understanding of historical . . . *possibility*' seriously). That 'explicit and ordered understanding' seems to foreclose on the nature of the 'actuality' it claims to understand—whatever the question is, it already knows the answer. Except that it doesn't really seem much of an answer in practice. The idea of 'historical actuality and possibility' which it lays claim to turns out to be endlessly deferred, and for good reason. For it is not really *historical* possibility: it is an affirmation of faith, a belief in some form of unalienated existence beyond exploitation—in fact, a familiar ideal of human flourishing, now projected into an unknowable future. The supposed 'grounding' of all that 'serious noticing' that makes up literary criticism could thus appear to take the form of an unredeemable IOU. That would, of course, be too flip as a way of understanding the eschatology through which Marx (and Lukács) linked the present to the future, but it at least suggests that we should not let the appeal to such a conception of 'historical possibility' pull rank when it comes to discriminating among various pieces of critical writing.

'In the Academic Counting-House'

Turning to Mulhern's most recent response to my work, the greater part of his 2020 essay 'In the Academic Counting-House' (now reproduced in this volume) gives a generous and often appreciative account of some of my recent writing about higher education policy, and, though I might challenge a particular emphasis here or there, it would be ungracious to cavil at such treatment. There are, however, a couple of issues which it is worth pursuing for what they say about our respective positions in this longer exchange. The first concerns the question of genre and therefore of audience. Wonderful though long analytical essays in *NLR* may be, they cannot be our only form of publication if we want to reach a range of audiences. *Speaking of Universities* was explicitly an assemblage of different literary forms written in different registers for different types of occasion or publication. The 'Open Letter to Liam Byrne', which Mulhern makes much of, was included to illustrate a minor variant, trying to engage the major opposition party at a particular political moment. In such an opportunist piece of writing, larger analyses would be out of place: what is needed are a small number of succinct points and a few practical suggestions. It's not a genre I like or have much indulged in, but it seemed right to include it as an example of a relevant different form, alongside op-ed columns, speeches, and other occasional compositions. It is placed in an appendix, along with these other ephemeral short pieces, because it is not an argued statement of my main case—in fact, it is one of the shortest pieces in the whole book, just three pages of Verso's generously laid-out text. The longer essays in the body of the book better represent its critical analysis of the received wisdom about higher education policy. There is, of course, a recurring dilemma for anyone attempting to make an intervention in contemporary public debate: stay too close to the conventional forms and one risks becoming more broadly complicit in established norms, but stray too far from these forms and one runs the contrary risk of failing to connect with the desired audiences at all.

Musing on this, I take some comfort from a passage in Mulhern's essay, 'Marxist Literary Criticism: Past and Future', where he says 'we cannot delude ourselves that there is, for now, life outside the dominant culture, but we might at least learn to maintain a critical distance from its passing absolutes'.[15] 'For now', I take it, holds out the hope of some kind of end of capitalism, and perhaps the absolutes are described as 'passing' in order to indicate that they are not as fixed or powerful as they like to think. Those are, no doubt, salutary reminders of the transience of all things, but, even with those qualifications in place, the sentiment, enjoining a severe realism about where we have to start from, suggests to me that we should not despise forms which, viewed from a loftier perspective, may seem tainted by association with a dominant consensus.

---

15 Mulhern, 'Marxist Literary Criticism: Past and Future', in *The Present Lasts a Long Time*, p. 53.

This relates to the second issue to be raised here, namely (to borrow a familiar formulation) 'What is to be done?' Mulhern notes the 'want of any point of collective political leverage' in my writing about universities, adding, 'In this lies the importance of developing concrete demands, both local and general, aimed at limiting and reversing the advance of the academic bureaucracy.'[16] We would, I assume, both agree that this is more easily said than done, but I don't see myself as having altogether abstained from attempts to tackle this problem. Over the past decade or more, I have touched on various possibilities, from altering the basis of funding for higher education to restoring some forms of academic self-governance, though I would not pretend that my work has proposed an elaborated plan of action (nor has anyone else's work, I would suggest). One traditional response would focus on trying to get the Labour Party to adopt some sensible policies for the future of universities. I don't discount this: however bad Labour may have been, the Tories have been a lot worse. I think it's a mistake among some self-described 'radical' critics to eschew mainstream national politics altogether, as all equally subordinate to capitalist imperatives. Moreover, some policies that are not directly about universities could nonetheless benefit them (such as limiting outsourcing and privatization of services, or ensuring proper legal enforcement of employment rights, things more likely under a Labour than a Tory government). Even so, Labour in recent years have shown little sign of thinking seriously about higher education, and I can't honestly say I expect much from this direction.

More promising, partly because more responsive to the concerns of academics, are moves to organize for greater self-government within universities. There are several things here that I've argued for over the years. One would be some version of the system that still prevails in many continental European systems whereby the rector and similar higher offices are filled by election. There are lots of questions here, especially about the extent of the electorate and whether there could be candidates not already members of the

---

16 'Counting-House', above, p. 175.

academic staff and so on, but the gains would, in my view, far outweigh the losses. Another, related, step would be for the roles of pro-vice-chancellors and deans to be filled by senior academics on a rotating basis; that's to say, they would hold the post for a fixed term and then revert to the ranks, rather than forming a separate cadre and career pattern, as is now largely the case in British universities. The advantages of this in terms of collegiality, knowledge of the issues, attention to academic values, and so on are obvious, though it would mean a lot of senior academics rethinking the blind pursuit of publication and external funding as the only career goals. A third step would be the revival of senates, as serious academic policy-making bodies (and not, as they are now, merely too-late-in-the-process reactive bodies, at best). And a fourth would be proper sector-wide conditions governing the position of non-permanent staff, including their involvement in decision-making. These are internal changes, and I recognize that they a) would involve some radical alterations to institutions' current functioning, and b) are mostly not easily to be achieved in the short term. Still, they are something to unite around and work for.

But the difficulties are formidable, and we have to be honest in admitting that these difficulties include the apathy and careerism of so many academics. In the course of the 2018 strike I spoke in several places about the larger context of the issues involved. It was encouraging to find numbers of academics (and students) not just engaged on behalf of the strike, but convinced that the experience had galvanized them and their colleagues on a wider range of issues, so that they were now resolved that matters on their campus could not return to the pre-strike status quo. It was, as I say, encouraging to meet this response, and I hope I did nothing to discourage it, but I did, and do, remain sceptical. I suspected that once all the usual processes of university business started up again, this energy would begin to dissipate, and the sheer power and intractability of the official machinery would drive colleagues to withdraw into their own teaching and research. I would certainly welcome the 'collective effort' that Mulhern calls for in his final sentence, but, as we both realize, simply calling for it won't make

it materialize. As so often, there can be a fine line separating resignation, which I don't believe I have lapsed into, from a realistic
acknowledgement of obstacles.

There is also an element of the division of labour involved. We
cannot each of us do everything, and if I can make any useful
contribution I'm pretty sure it's by writing—writing to identify
and draw attention to what's happening, writing in more than one
genre, writing as someone moderately well informed about the
past as well as the present of universities, writing as a scholar who
can bring at least some of the resources of history, literature, and
philosophy to bear on the topic. This, it seems to me, is the task of
criticism. That task is, needless to say, not the only thing; at some
moments it may not even seem like the most urgent or consequential thing; but it is one worthwhile and often essential thing. Others
have greater talents than I do for different forms of organization
and activism; I don't underestimate the value of such activities,
but I think it's best I stick to my last. The positive things Francis
Mulhern says about my polemics over higher education policy
encourage me now to propose that selection of my writing as one
illustration—necessarily a limited and local one—of the kind of
cultural criticism for which I was trying to make a space in more
general, impersonal terms in our earlier exchanges.

Naming

There is a well-known distinction, mostly applied (it seems) to
historians, between the 'lumpers' and the 'splitters'. The working
idea looks simple enough. Lumpers are those whose intellectual
instinct is to bring things together, to look for common factors in
disparate materials, to seek underlying patterns or large-scale
causes. Splitters, by contrast, are drawn to discriminating, to identifying significant differences among ostensibly similar elements,
to respecting the quiddity of distinct phenomena. Any reference to
this contrast is usually quickly followed up with an affirmation
that historians (and others) need to combine the virtues of each
group: we cannot master the infinite multitudinousness of the past
without using concepts and categories that are the lumpers'

stock-in-trade, while at the same time we need to be constantly
alert to the differences hiding under an initial appearance of simi-
larity. That eirenic moral having been drawn, historians (and
others) are then generally content to go their own ways, lumping
and splitting as circumstances or temperaments dictate.

In my view, the most important and most obvious thing to be
said about this distinction—though I have never seen it said elsewhere—is that, as usually stated, it is not some neutral report or
impartial overview: the terms of the distinction are lumpers' categories. The very act of dividing up the relevant population into
two large, mutually exclusive and apparently exhaustive groups is
already a validation of the procedures that are said to be constitutive of one of the two categories. Of course, in making this point,
one risks seeming a little leaden-footed: surely, it may be said, this
is just a handy heuristic or, more colloquially, a bit of light-hearted
banter, a distinction with just enough truth in it to be interesting
but not something to be pursued in too literal or earnest a spirit.
But, as we know from countless other forms of experience, pinning
labels on people can have real consequences, and we are often
disinclined to find it an adequate response or defence to say that it
was 'just a bit of banter'.

I found myself thinking of this familiar distinction as I reread
the earlier instalments of our exchange. Perhaps I may begin by
returning to the one moment in that exchange where I felt that
Mulhern's normally sure touch deserted him. I can still recall my
sense of puzzlement and even dismay that a writer of Mulhern's
quality should essay a point that was not just wrong but seemed
to me obviously wrong-headed, implausible, even a kind of category mistake. He proposed at one point that my style of cultural
criticism was 'at one with the times' in being 'another kind of
privatization'.[17] It was almost as though someone eager to align
my writing with one of the dominant strands in contemporary
politics had turned what was at best a pretty strained analogical
resemblance into a revelation of fundamental identity. At the

---

17 'The Logic of Cultural Criticism', above, p. 113; I registered my dismay in a
footnote in 'On Variousness', above, p. 138.

time, I did not feel inclined to make much of this, there being so many other more interesting, and more positive, features of Mulhern's work to engage with (and he has made handsome amends in his recent discussion of my work[18]), but that moment came back to me as I read the concluding paragraphs of 'In the Academic Counting-House' because they, too, seemed tinged with a similar urge to place me on a map of contemporary political identities. Perhaps I had better say immediately that I am not here engaging in some quixotic enterprise of trying to rid our discourses of all political labels: they are often convenient and sometimes indispensable. The question is, rather, why does the desire to settle upon some such classification seem to be accorded such priority over other characterizations that it threatens to push aside all the careful discussion that has gone before, rather as though a delicately wrought piece of music felt compelled to conclude with the emphatic repetition of a couple of simple chords?

The distinction between 'lumpers' and 'splitters' calls to mind—perhaps is even a restatement of—the old joke about there being two kinds of people: those who divide the world up into two kinds of people and those who don't. The logical recursiveness is, needless to say, meant to be part of the joke. But the formula exhibits a more general truth. Being classified as one of those who 'don't' only has meaning in the context of whether one is or isn't a member of the group who divide people into two kinds. The language and classification of the first group are dominant, even coercive. But why should we think *that* position has any logical or practical priority? Why not start, and finish, by thinking about the diversity of types of people in other terms? There is a point to this objection which is not merely the reflex of a kind of fastidious nominalism. In binary schemes of classification, it is easy for those in the second category to end up being defined in terms of their culpable lack of the properties exhibited by those in the first category, as those classed as, say, 'non-white' have long understood. No one could sensibly dispense with all categories, but it is often

---

18 'Counting-House', above, Chapter 7.

a legitimate, and even valuable, objection, faced with a particular grid, to say, 'I wouldn't start from there.'

I risk labouring this point not because I want to repeat a central theme of our earlier exchanges, but because a particular form of such binarism now seems entrenched in much Left discourse, with even Mulhern's careful formulations not being altogether exempt from it. From the endlessly shifting kaleidoscope of language use, I want to pick out a usage which seems to have become very common in Left academic circles in recent decades, namely a sweeping and politically pejorative sense of 'liberalism'. For the sake of economy, let me cite an example which I have commented on elsewhere, Joseph North's 2017 book, *Literary Criticism: A Concise Political History*. As I remarked in my review of his book:

> North uses the term [liberalism] with striking freedom, though it is hard not to feel that in recent years it has become almost unusable unless prefaced by elaborate definitional preliminaries. In so far as I can chart any consistency in North's usage, 'liberal' does not refer to any of the traditional understandings of political liberalism, yet nor does it follow the usage of current US politics in denoting anything to the left of the dominant right-wing orthodoxy. Instead, the nearest synonym I can supply would be 'not Marxist'. North frequently condemns figures who were 'liberals rather than leftists' and he seems to make 'liberalism' and 'leftism' pretty much exhaustive of the political possibilities, at least in English studies. When he refers to 'the left-liberal mainstream of the discipline', the implied contrast appears to be with 'leftism'. At one point he speaks of 'the left proper' as 'those whose commitment to equality runs beyond the boundaries set by the liberal consensus', and at another he refers to 'liberalism's failure to admit the determination of the superstructure by the base'. It is hard to make the important discriminations while relying on this vocabulary: such prodigal use of 'liberal' becomes a night in which all (non-Marxist) cows are black . . .

Even a writer as sophisticated as North does not quite escape that irritating manner in which those who, in the course of itemizing the failings of various approaches, lump them together as 'liberal' and then assert, rather airily, that these defects would all be remedied if we undertook a properly 'materialist' criticism. But we never learn what exactly this would be like in practice: those who claim to possess this key to the universe are always in the position of implying that, for the moment, they've left it in their other jacket.[19]

It is hard not to feel that the main justification for choosing the label is its putatively pejorative force. There are two kinds of people: those who understand and endorse historical materialism and . . . liberals.

Mulhern is an exceptionally careful and scrupulous writer, but I find myself ruminating on this wider usage when he speaks of my 'cultural liberalism', and concludes that the most 'telling description' of my position would be 'liberal-socialism', and especially when he observes: 'Collini remains averse to political self-classification, in a familiar liberal reflex.'[20] If 'liberal' in this last case simply meant those who are averse to political self-classification, then one might be inclined to let it pass as circular. But, of course, it brings a much larger baggage-train of implication with it: not only does it signify 'not sufficiently radical', but, by association or subliminally, it brings with it the suggestion of affiliation to a particular kind of political and economic order. In reaction to this, I find myself wanting to ask: who gets to do the naming? Who gets to decide that identifying someone's alleged 'political orientation' outranks or overrides other characterizations, including their self-characterization? What warrant does the lumper have for corralling everyone else under the label of 'splitters'? My point here, as elsewhere, is obviously not an objection to the processes of description and classification as such, but a wish

---

19   Joseph North, *Literary Criticism: A Concise Political History*, Cambridge, MA, 2017, pp. 76, 146, 116, 8, 37; see my analysis in 'A Lot to Be Said', *London Review of Books*, 2 November 2017. Mulhern expressed some reservations about North's argument in an otherwise generally positive review: 'Critical Revolutions', *New Left Review* 110, March–April 2018, pp. 39–54.

20   'Counting-House', above, p. 173.

to slow those processes down, to warn against some of the easy slippages buried in familiar terms, and to challenge labels that have become misleading or tendentious. In my view, the sense of 'liberal' that I have been discussing belongs in this last category.

Intellectual controversy may often involve some unconscious self-quotation, so let me make that process conscious at this point. Attempting to do justice (in my 2013 Introduction to the new edition of *Two Cultures?*) to Leavis's much-maligned literary tactics in his attack on C. P. Snow, I flirted with pastiche in describing one conception of the role of cultural criticism.

> Stipulative definition of abstract terms is of very little value— indeed it may get in the way of deeper thinking—even though one's opponents may demand that one's position be given crisp and definitive formulation. Instead, the cultural critic cultivates and, by example and even by irritating obstructiveness, incites others to cultivate, a restless dissatisfaction with abstract terms, a mindful awareness of the reductive or Procrustean potential of all general formulations. This is, or should be, home territory for the literary critic, and points to a distinctive role in public debate—or at least, to a form of engagement in which a more than ordinary attentiveness to language functions not as a distracting fastidiousness, but as the active embodiment of positive values and the only way such values can be made effective in controversy.[21]

At their best, Mulhern's steely analyses take one route to jolting us out of lazily accepted terminology; my sceptical dwelling on variousness takes another.

Forbidding Mourning

In rereading some of the essays in *The Present Lasts a Long Time*, one of the things that strikes me is how early Mulhern's basic

---

21   Stefan Collini, 'Introduction', to F. R. Leavis, *Two Cultures? The Significance of C. P. Snow*, Cambridge 2013, p. 15.

political orientation was formed.[22] He speaks of his radical commitments as a seventeen-year-old entering University College Dublin; he was sufficiently advanced in both his thinking and his commitment to become an editor at *NLR* at twenty-three; he published *The Moment of 'Scrutiny'*, in which the outlines of so much of his later thinking can be glimpsed, at the age of twenty-seven. It makes for an impressive story of political seriousness. He has, as is amply evident from his writing, gone on developing, gone on thinking, but the main lines along which that development and that thinking have proceeded are visible strikingly early.

By contrast, I cannot claim an early radical political identity because I cannot claim any early political identity at all. My younger adult years were taken up with my private existential efforts to grow up a little after a socially and emotionally limiting childhood, with the result that I was culpably neglectful of the public world around me. In my twenties and early thirties, I was attempting to establish an academic career along more or less conventional lines while being under-attentive to contemporary politics. Thereafter, that career became a little less conventional, involving a certain amount of border-crossing or category-blurring. My earliest work was in intellectual history, especially the history of social and political thought; that mutated into a concern with various forms of cultural criticism and the public roles of writers and other intellectuals, while much of my recent scholarly work has focused on the history of literary criticism. In terms of genres of writing, too, there has been a certain amount of movement, from orthodox academic monographs to more interpretive or synoptic essays and shorter forms, and on to several kinds of literary journalism, especially long review-essays, for journals such as the *London Review of Books* and the *Times Literary Supplement*. And although I wrote some pieces that were highly critical of current developments in higher education policy as early as the mid 1980s, it is only really within the last fifteen or twenty years that I have attempted any sustained engagement in public debate.

---

22   I touched briefly on this contrast in 'On Variousness', penultimate sentence, p. 131.

I mention these facts, unremarkable enough in themselves, in order to highlight the ways in which my and Mulhern's different trajectories have informed and partly shaped our exchanges. My writing has not been held together from the beginning by a clear sense of political purpose in the way that his has; it has also been both more disparate in subject-matter and more changeable over time. (The fact that the earliest piece republished in *Into the Mêlée* dates from 1981, even though that piece had already been republished in *The Present Lasts a Long Time*, is surely expressive of his own sense of the deep continuity of his concerns and responses.[23]) Within the practice of intellectual history, it is a delicate matter to decide how much consistency a body of work written over several decades should be expected to display, or how much things written in one genre and set of circumstances may fairly be used to indicate settled dispositions across the board. Given my own uneven history, I would naturally like commentators to exercise considerable caution in choosing passages from my earlier work to document my views in the present.

Yet, for all the differences of our respective formations, our intellectual identities are not in other ways so far apart. As this brief overview suggests, I have long found myself straddling or crossing the border between intellectual history and literary criticism, endeavours which, as I understand them, are not utterly distinct in intellectual terms, but which have quite separate institutional identities in British universities. When, after moving from being a member of the Intellectual History Subject-Group at Sussex to a post in the Faculty of English at Cambridge, I was promoted and had to choose a title for my Readership (and subsequently Professorship), I chose 'Intellectual History and English Literature'. At the time, it was, I could be pretty sure, the only such title in British academia, rather an odd one to many ears. So it was with a jolt, both of surprise and the recognition of a kind of

---

23   This essay first appeared as the Introduction to Régis Debray, *Teachers, Writers, Celebrities*, London 1981; it was reprinted, under the title 'Intelligentsias and Their Histories', in *The Present Lasts a Long Time*, pp. 70–84; it is reprinted again, now entitled 'Teachers, Writers, Celebrities', in *Into the Mêlée*, pp. 1–19.

kinship, that many years later I noticed Mulhern's byline giving his post at Middlesex as 'English Literature and Intellectual History'. The publication of *Into the Mêlée* underlines our affinities: it is not just that there are essays on a number of figures and themes which I have also written about—Leavis, Empson, Williams, Orwell, Hobsbawm, intellectuals, cultural journals— but that, at a deeper level, there is a similar preoccupation with the literary strategies of the more intellectually serious forms of public debate and a similar taste for the essay-length appraisal of a figure or a journal in the round. Despite our very different starting points, our tracks do seem to keep crossing and re-crossing.

Let me end with a more 'playful' note, and then a final declaration.[24] A friend who is an ardent Arsenal fan has over the years instructed me in the first and most important consideration one should always bring to bear on any matter to do with football: is it bad for Spurs? My friend imparts this cardinal principle with infinite layers of self-irony and sophistication, but it's also a way of teasing me about my culpable lack of the appropriate form of tribalism. I sometimes wonder whether Francis Mulhern has set himself to play a somewhat similar role in relation to my cultural criticism. I can appreciate the force of the Schmittian insistence that politics is about friends and foes without concluding that that's all there is to be said about politics, or that politics is all there is to be said about life. I can't imagine that Mulhern would disagree with those propositions, expressed in that trite form, but I sense that he feels I spend too much time sitting on the fence or preening myself on the fineness of my discriminations, and that he wants to flush out which team I, in the end, support. Predictably, I can't help feeling that, although there are circumstances in which that is a relevant and pressing question, it's not always and everywhere the most interesting question.

Instead, a recurring preoccupation of my work, as I see it, is the attempt to deploy forms of understanding and expression that are adequate to the scale and scope of the matter in hand. When we

24 Mulhern at one point describes my critical resources as 'playful as well as "pin-striped"'; 'Counting-House', above, p. 157.

are trying to understand the large-scale transformations of econo-
mies and societies across many centuries, the Marxist tradition
may provide some of the most illuminating and compelling
resources we have. When we are trying to understand modulations
in the prose of an individual writer, we need, in my view, to look
principally to other idioms and approaches. Many forms of
cultural criticism may fall between these extremes, requiring difficult judgements about the most appropriate mode. Though I have,
over time, come more and more to recognize the immense power
of capital in the present, and have become increasingly committed
to a socialist politics as a result, nonetheless I so often find that
scholars working within a broadly Marxist inspiration move *too
quickly* from the general categories to the individual instance. A
great deal of theoretical labour has been expended within that
tradition in the attempt to plot 'forms of determination' or those
intermediate processes through which the shaping power of the
mode of production is assumed to operate in the intellectual and
cultural sphere. That is necessary and worthwhile theoretical
work, but the pay-off when it comes to understanding the kinds of
thing that interest me in the literary and intellectual past mostly
seems either implausibly reductive or disappointingly slight.
Categories that derive from a scheme designed to comprehend
major long-term social changes often turn out to be, in my view,
clumsy instruments when applied to the fine grain of local understanding or criticism. Of course, we all make choices about how
far back to stand from that fine-grained detail: no intellectually
serious enterprise simply reproduces it. In addition, there is a
recognizable political case for saying that priority should be given
to trying to understand the large-scale phenomena that affect
most people's lives—questions of population, production, power,
the environment, and so on, addressed on a global and transhistorical scale. *NLR* has a proud tradition of encouraging such
intellectual ambitiousness and absence of parochialism. But other
things are also worth doing, and as it happens Mulhern has mostly
chosen to work on more specific aspects of British intellectual and
literary culture from the last 150 years, which is where we coincide
and can therefore fruitfully differ.

There can be no 'last word' about an exchange such as ours, and anyway others will in time have their own words to add. But, in stopping for the moment even if not concluding, I will, risking the bathos of the self-evident, say that the Left should not shy away from debates on these topics or regard them as of minor or peripheral importance. The very category 'the Left' may seem to reinforce the priority of the political, but it will be clear that I think this is exactly where we need to tread carefully. Enlarging our understanding and promoting our politics are two enterprises, not one, however intimate the connections between them. Francis Mulhern has given us some outstanding examples of critical work that is powerfully informed by a particular political commitment, but I want to make a little more space for other approaches, idioms, and responses to come into play. I don't think that weakens or betrays our politics; quite the contrary. If drawing on other resources to enlarge our understanding in this way is seen as a threat to our politics, then there's something wrong with our politics.

Index